BEFORE
CHRISTMAS

BEFORE CHRISTMAS

The Story of Jesus

FROM THE BEGINNING OF TIME
TO THE MANGER

Bill Crowder

Requests for permission to quote from this book should be directed to: Permissions
Department, Our Daily Bread Publishing, PO Box 3566, Grand Rapids, MI 49501, or
contact us by email at permissionsdept@odb.org.

Scripture quotations, unless otherwise indicated, are from the New American Standard
Bible®, copyright © 1960, 1962, 1963, 1968, 1971, 1972, 1973, 1975, 1977, 1995 by The
Lockman Foundation. Used by permission. (Lockman.org)

Scripture quotations marked NKJV are from the New King James Version®. Copyright ©
1982 by Thomas Nelson. Used by permission. All rights reserved.

Interior design by Beth Shagene

Library of Congress Cataloging-in-Publication Data

Names: Crowder, Bill, author.
Title: Before Christmas : the story of Jesus from the beginning of time to the manger /
    Bill Crowder.
Description: Grand Rapids : Discovery House, 2019. | Summary: "This intriguing book
    will take you behind the story of the Savior's birth to help you see and know Christ
    in a way that leads to greater wonder and appreciation. Discover what the Bible says
    about the One who came into the world--before He came into the world"-- Provided
    by publisher.
Identifiers: LCCN 2019022674 | ISBN 9781627079570 (paperback)
Subjects: LCSH: Jesus Christ--Person and offices. | Jesus Christ--Nativity.
Classification: LCC BT203 .C76 2019 | DDC 232/.8--dc23
LC record available at https://lccn.loc.gov/2019022674

Printed in the United States of America

21 22 23 24 25 26 27 / 9 8 7 6 5 4 3

To the memory of

G. Campbell Morgan
(1863–1945)

A pastor and teacher who has pastored my life
with his writings and who taught me
how to read the Scriptures
with fresh eyes and an expectant heart.

Contents

Acknowledgments   *9*

Introduction: The Christmas Backstory   *11*

1. His Character as God   *15*

2. His Relationship with the Father   *39*

3. His Preparation for the Cross   *59*

4. His Role as Creator   *79*

5. His Appearances in the Old Testament   *99*

6. His Announced Arrival   *119*

Conclusion: The Christmas Story   *141*

Notes   *145*

Acknowledgments

As the subtitle suggests, this is a book about the story behind the narrative of Christmas—the backstory, if you will. But here at the outset of this endeavor, it is important for you to know that there is also a backstory to this book. I never cease to be amazed at both the privilege of writing and the encouraging support I receive from a community of friends who come together to make a book like this happen. My deep gratitude goes to the team at Discovery House and the wonderful encouragement and help they provide. Ken Petersen (publisher), Miranda Gardner, Dave Branon, Meaghan Minkus, and more have contributed to bringing this project to the light of day. I am profoundly grateful for the privilege of working with such great people and professionals.

Of course, there is a backstory to my life as well. My personal backstory begins with parents (Earl and

Bee Crowder) and siblings (Linda, Rob, Dave, Carole, Kathy, and Scott) who always made Christmas worth celebrating and who, along the way, pointed me to my need of Christ. For friends and teachers in Bible college who nudged me toward ministry and opened doors of opportunity for learning and experimentation in teaching, I am also thankful. At home, my wife, Marlene, has walked this journey with me for more than four decades, with our kids (Matt, Beth, Steve, Andy, and Mark) joining one by one. At times, a life in ministry has been more difficult than we could ever imagine, yet at other times it has been more blessed than we could ever deserve. My family has hung in there and helped smooth out the rough spots with love and humor. I am grateful.

And, ultimately, to the real reason and purpose for this book—Jesus the Christ. His coming at Bethlehem to be our Redeemer is still the best story of all. Exploring the backstory of the God who became flesh and dwelt among us is an exploration worth embracing. I'm honored to have the privilege of trying to tell it.

The Christmas Backstory

For the length of our marriage, my wife, Marlene, has hoped that someday I would become handy. To that end, we spend a disproportionate amount of time watching things like *This Old House*, *Property Brothers*, *Fixer Upper*, and more. And more. And more. Learning a bit here and a bit there from watching others renovate and improve houses has been the most tangible result of watching those programs. But there's a catch to that learning experience—you have to understand the *before* of that old house before you can appreciate what can lead to the *after*.

The same thing is true in many of the life stories we encounter. The famous actor who was a roofing installer before making it big on the silver screen. The athlete who endured the darkness of urban blight but went on to become a superstar and philanthropist. The newscaster who battled with dyslexia and overcame it to become a trusted journalist. Stories like these abound—but the context of the backstory makes all the difference in appreciating the power of the story we now see.

In infinitely more important ways, this same reality applies to the Christmas story. I have felt for years that when we enter the Christmas story, we enter it too late. We consider Jesus's coming, but we forget that He had to leave where He was to come to where we are. We are so thrilled by the baby in the manger that we don't pause to remember who that baby is. We forget that the eternal Son of God left the Father's presence, which He had known and enjoyed since before time began, in order to become—amazingly—that baby in that manger.

This should take our breath away! It should cause us to ponder the glory He left and to contemplate the darkness into which He came. Think of the perfect relationship He left behind to embrace the brokenness that our rebellion had inflicted upon His creation. And think of the privileges and positions He set aside so He could come to serve—when in reality He deserved to be served.

This is the backstory of the Christmas story, and I invite you to join me in attempting to explore that backstory in these pages. While the Bible does not give us volumes of insight on the Christmas backstory, neither is it silent. We are told enough to cause us to marvel at the sacrifices Christ made to come to earth and become our sacrificial Lamb—the One who rescued us from death. That is why the Christmas backstory is so important. It adds eternal value to the coming of Jesus by unveiling His truest identity.

This is a journey worth taking. But it is more than just a learning exercise to fill in the blanks of our theological knowledge. It is a journey into the very heart of God and the Son of His love. It is a journey to understand what it really means that "the Father has sent the Son to be the Savior of the world" (1 John 4:14). Join me on the journey.

1

His Character
as God

From all eternity—long before His birth—
Jesus was equal to the Father.
In every way, Jesus was and is God.

Emily Elizabeth Steele Elliott was the daughter of an Anglican clergyman living in Victorian England in the late 1800s. Heavily involved in what we today would call outreach ministries, she served in a children's Sunday school program that was partially involved in reaching at-risk kids from the streets of the darker sides of London.

As the Christmas season approached one year, Emily wanted to communicate the message of Jesus's birth in a way that would help these largely unchurched kids understand who Jesus is and why He came. Given her pedigree (the niece of Charlotte Elliott, author of the hymn "Just as I Am"), it is not surprising that her instinct was to write a song to help the children. For her song, she wisely understood that Christmas has a backstory, so she resisted the urge to begin her lyrics with the baby in the manger. Instead, she started the narrative much earlier, writing:

> Thou didst leave Thy throne and Thy kingly
>   crown,
> When Thou camest to earth for me;
> But in Bethlehem's home was there found
>   no room
> For Thy holy nativity.

While those words may seem stiff and outdated to our ears, it is fascinating to remember that they were originally penned for the ears of children. What is amazing is that not only was this intended to be a kids' Sunday school song but it also acknowledged a profound idea—the Christmas story didn't begin in Nazareth. Nor did it begin in Bethlehem. Its backstory started in eternity past in the Father's presence.

The key in her opening lyric is the word *leave*, because it shows us what He *left* in order to come *here*. From eternity past this had been His state and position, and it reveals to us where He was and how He had been honored. It opens a door ever so slightly for us to see Jesus's backstory. And it exposes for us not only where He was but also who He was. He was God.

Why is this so important? A. W. Tozer wrote:

> What comes into our minds when we think about God is the most important thing about us.
>
> The history of mankind will probably show that no people has ever risen above its religion, and man's spiritual history will positively demonstrate that no religion has ever been greater than its idea of God. Worship is pure or base, as the worshiper entertains high or low thoughts about God.
>
> For this reason, the gravest question before the church is always God Himself, and the most portentous fact about any man is not what he at a given time may say or do, but what he in his deep heart conceives God to be like.[1]

That perspective also applies to our understanding of the Christ of Christmas, and the only way to rightly

understand Him is to see Him as more than a baby
in the manger. We would do well to see Him as the
eternal One who came in the flesh. Who, then, was
He—before He came? To see that, we need to see that
the apostle Paul's unique telling of the incarnation in
Philippians 2 explains the values that were reflected
in Emily Elliott's hymn. As she began the story in the
throne room of heaven, Paul also starts an eternity ago
in the Father's presence. He gives us four characteristics of Jesus as God:

1. *The God Who Serves*: "Have this attitude in
   yourselves which was also in Christ Jesus"
   (Philippians 2:5).

2. *The God Who Departed—and Arrived*: "Christ
   Jesus, who, although He existed in the form of
   God . . ." (Philippians 2:6a)

3. *The God Who Sacrifices*: ". . . did not regard
   equality with God a thing to be grasped . . ."
   (Philippians 2:6b)

4. *The God Who Empties Himself*: ". . . but emptied
   Himself, taking the form of a bond-servant,
   and being made in the likeness of men"
   (Philippians 2:7).

The God Who Serves (Philippians 2:5)

As my time teaching at a Bible college was coming to an end, I had already begun serving a small church congregation as their pastor. To have proper accreditation, I applied for ordination—a grueling process of preparation and testing to determine whether or not I was orthodox in my theology before being endorsed for ministry. The day before my ordination examination—which would be a three-hour grilling by a dozen Bible and theology professors—I was given a heads-up about a certain doctrine. I was urged to study what theologians refer to as the "kenosis theory" (found in Philippians 2), because one of the profs on the panel always asked about it.

That warning launched me into a cram session on one of the most challenging and important truths found anywhere in the Bible. It is also an example of the great contrasts we see in the truths of the Bible. Philippians 2:5–11, which is complex and challenging theologically, is believed to have been taken from an ancient hymn! What a contrast—dense theology married with simple worship.

Have this attitude in yourselves which was also in Christ Jesus, who, although He existed in the form of God, did not regard equality with God a thing to be grasped, but emptied Himself, taking the form of a bond-servant, and being made in the likeness of men. Being found in appearance as a man, He humbled Himself by becoming obedient to the point of death, even death on a cross. For this reason also, God highly exalted Him, and bestowed on Him the name which is above every name, so that at the name of Jesus EVERY KNEE WILL BOW, of those who are in heaven and on earth and under the earth, and that every tongue will confess that Jesus Christ is Lord, to the glory of God the Father.

The "kenosis theory" reflects Paul's statement that Christ "emptied Himself" (v. 7). Later we will look at this kenosis theory in more depth, but first we must see its context. The context is that as God's children we are urged to exhibit the "mind" that was seen in Jesus himself (v. 5). What is that mind? First, it is not about mental acumen or intellectual capacity. The word *mind* can also be translated "attitude," "perspective," or "character." Perhaps, as in the New International

Version, the best way to translate it would be "mind-set." It speaks of an approach to life that saturates everything we say and do.

So, what was and is the mind-set of Christ? At its core the mind of Christ is a servant's heart born out of a self-sacrificial spirit. Notice our Savior's own words:

- "For even the Son of Man did not come to be served, but to serve, and to give His life a ransom for many" (Mark 10:45).

- "For I gave you an example that you also should do as I did to you" (John 13:15); Jesus made this statement *after* washing the disciples' feet, taking to himself the role of the lowest servant of the household!

- "No one has taken [My life] away from Me, but I lay it down on My own initiative" (John 10:18).

If we are to develop a servant's heart, we must follow His example. We must not live in our own mind-set, attitude, or character, but in "the mind of Christ." To that end, Paul opened his discussion of the kenosis, and the Christmas backstory it represents, by saying: "Let this mind be in you which was also in Christ Jesus" (Philippians 2:5 NKJV).

How did that happen? How did Christ exhibit both the heart of a servant and a willingness to sacrifice self? He did this by setting aside His home in heaven to come to where we are. And He did so by setting aside His divine rights and privileges as He left the Father's presence to come to us as the God who serves.

The God Who Departed—and Arrived
(Philippians 2:6a)

See again what Emily Elliott wrote in her children's hymn:

> Thou didst leave Thy throne and Thy kingly
> crown,
> When Thou camest to earth for me;
> But in Bethlehem's home was there found no
> room
> For Thy holy nativity.

One website that focuses on the study of hymns points out the clear pattern Elliott employed in her song. Each verse begins with a positive and ends with a negative, with the two pieces connected by the word *but*. Here the past glory of the eternal presence of the Godhead is pictured in the throne and crown that Christ left. That glory is placed in contrast to the absence of a place for the One who "came to His own, and His own did not receive Him" (John 1:11 NKJV). The pivots of light versus darkness and relationship versus rejection make for brilliant songwriting.

This, however, is so much more than just a clever song lyric. It is an idea that is essential not just to the Christmas story but to the entire biblical story as well. The thought that Christ had to *leave* something else in order to come here is what the apostle Paul captured when he wrote Philippians 2:5–6: "Christ Jesus, who, although He existed in the form of God . . . ."

This statement confronts us with an idea of tremendous significance: "He existed in the form of God." This clause speaks of a reality that was true before time began. Before the creation of the universe. Before the collapse of the human race with the Fall. Notice a couple of words that are critical to our exploration of the person of Christ: *existed* and *form*.

Existed. The first important word is *existed*, which is the translation of the Greek *huparcho*. This term conveys great strength, because it has two significant implications. As I type the word *implications*, I hear the voice of the late "Teacher of Preachers" Haddon

Robinson whispering in my ear. Haddon consistently reminded us that we can't just speak of implications in broad, undefined terms. We have to be honest with the biblical text and honest with ourselves, asking:

- Is this a *necessary* implication (what the text *must* mean),

- a *probable* implication (what it *could* mean),

- or just a *possible* implication (what it *might* mean)?

Given the context of the story Paul is telling, I am convinced that the implications are not merely possible or even probable—they are *necessary* implications of the word *existed*.

The first implication is that Christ existed *prior* to His conception in Mary's womb. The necessity of this preexistence is found in John 1:1, which tells us, "In the beginning was the Word, and the Word was with God, and the Word was God." The "Word" of John 1:1 (*logos*) is clearly the Christ, because verse 14 tells us that this Word "became flesh, and dwelt among us." The apostle Paul takes it even further in Colossians 1:17, writing, "He [Christ] is before all things, and in Him all things hold together." There can be

no question that when Paul says that Christ existed in
the form of God, this concept embraces real, genuine
preexistence.

The second implication is that *huparcho* not only
teaches *prior* existence but it also speaks of *eternal* existence. It is not just that Christ *is*—but that He *was* and
He forever *will be*. This necessary implication is also
confirmed in the Scriptures as Micah 5:2 prophetically
spoke of Christ, saying, "His goings forth are from
long ago, from the days of eternity." The risen Jesus
personally made the claim of eternal existence when
He said to the apostle John, "I am the Alpha and the
Omega, . . . who is and who was and who is to come,
the Almighty" (Revelation 1:8).

As challenging as it is for us finite people to grasp,
Jesus did not just show up in Bethlehem. He did not
just come into being when conceived by the Holy
Spirit in Mary. He came into His earthly experience
from somewhere else—somewhere He had been from
all eternity past in the presence of the Father.

Form. The second key word in Philippians 2:6 is *form*.
It is another critical word in Paul's Christmas story.
Form is the English translation of the Greek word
morphe, and it can feel counterintuitive to us. When

we hear the word *form*, our tendency is to think about shape or external appearance. For example, in construction, forms are used in pouring concrete foundations, and those forms give the footings or foundations shape. Similarly, a *dress form* is a specially made female torso for dressmakers to use in making garments. These examples cause us to think about shape when we consider the word *form*.

However, *morphe* goes much deeper than surface shapes. It stresses the inner essence or reality of something, not the outward appearance. It is an expression that captures the idea of "being." By saying that in eternity past Christ existed in the "form" of God, Paul is expressing in the strongest possible terms the complete and absolute deity of Jesus Christ. Jesus is not *like* God—He *is* God. He does not *picture* deity—He *possesses* deity. This idea is clearly evident in Hebrews 1:3:

> He is the radiance of His glory and the exact representation of His nature, and upholds all things by the word of His power. When He had made purification of sins, He sat down at the right hand of the Majesty on high.

The key phrase is "the exact representation of His [God's] nature." The Bible teaches us that "God is spirit" (John 4:24), and as such He is hidden from our sight. The only way we could see the "essence" of God would be if that essence arrived in visible form. This means that in eternity past and in His incarnation, Christ was the very form, or essence, of God. In fact, John makes it clear that while we see the cross and resurrection as the primary reason Jesus came, there was more. He also came so we could see, in human flesh, the essence and nature of God: "No one has seen God at any time; the only begotten God who is in the bosom of the Father, He has explained Him" (John 1:18).

Only God could be (or come) in the form of God, and Jesus claimed that very thing for himself, as we see in John 5:18, "For this reason therefore the Jews were seeking all the more to kill Him, because He not only was breaking the Sabbath, but also was calling God His own Father, making Himself equal with God." Christ was fully and completely God in eternity past, and He displayed that perfect God-ness on the Mount of Transfiguration when the veil of flesh was lowered and the glory of Christ was displayed. That scene caused Simon Peter to write:

> For we did not follow cleverly devised tales when we made known to you the power and coming of our Lord Jesus Christ, but we were eyewitnesses of His majesty. For when He received honor and glory from God the Father, such an utterance as this was made to Him by the Majestic Glory, "This is My beloved Son with whom I am well-pleased"—and we ourselves heard this utterance made from heaven when we were with Him on the holy mountain. (2 Peter 1:16–18)

The apostle John added His own version when he wrote: "And the Word became flesh, and dwelt among us, and we saw His glory, glory as of the only begotten from the Father, full of grace and truth" (John 1:14).

Here we are reminded of the eternal nature of Christ as the second person of the Trinity. We see the eternal reality of Jesus's equality with the Father in John 17:5, where the Savior prayed: "Now, Father, glorify Me together with Yourself, with the glory which I had with You before the world was."

This, however, is not just a rehashing of orthodox theology. It is far more personal and far more critical. Critical to the Christmas story is the declaration that, far from being just another baby, the Christ was God in human flesh. This is the necessary truth of the incarnation of Jesus, fulfilling the prophecy of Isaiah 7:14, which Matthew affirms in Matthew 1:22–23:

> Now all this took place to fulfill what was spoken by the Lord through the prophet: "BEHOLD, THE VIRGIN SHALL BE WITH CHILD AND SHALL BEAR A SON, AND THEY SHALL CALL HIS NAME IMMANUEL," which translated means, "GOD WITH US."

Only if Jesus is truly God could He come to earth and be Immanuel—God with us. For the mission and message of Christ to make any sense at all, we must begin by seeing Him not only as the Son of God but also as God the Son.

However, all of that matters little if Christ had not been willing to lay aside that heavenly place and position. His mission in coming for us was in the very least a mission of self-sacrifice—laying His life down for us on the cross. As such, it shouldn't surprise us that this sacrifice did not begin on the cross or even in Bethlehem. Christ began that sacrifice by willingly giving up what was His so He could take hold of us. What else would we expect from the God who serves?

The God Who Sacrifices (Philippians 2:6b)

What was Jesus's position and condition in eternity past? He was God the Son, dwelling perfectly forever in the presence of the Father. Yet, as the true Servant His attitude about His status and position was one of giving away, not grasping it firmly. Notice Paul's next words in Philippians 2, which indicate that Jesus "did not regard equality with God a thing to be grasped" (v. 6).

What does that mean? The word translated *grasped* has a couple of meanings, and these meanings reflect the common ways we translate that word into English:

- A thing to be seized unlawfully (translated by the King James Version and the New King James Version as "robbery")

- A treasure to be selfishly clutched or clung to (translated by the New International Version and the New American Standard Bible as "grasped")

The context lets us see this refusal to use His status for his own benefit as part of Christ's perfect humility. It speaks of the attitude of Christ *before* He came into the world—that He would not selfishly cling to the privileges or prerogatives of His divine position. So, as the ultimate Servant He was willing to be utterly selfless—not clinging to what was rightfully His—so He could come into the world for you and for me. That was His heart, and that is His example, His attitude, and His mind-set.

Jesus did not cling to the privileges of His equality with the Father—and this is also the point of the Bible's most familiar verse, John 3:16. "God so loved the world" that He sent Jesus from the Father's presence to our broken, desperate world. But what Paul wants to add to that sending is that for Jesus to *come* He first had to *leave*. In doing that, Jesus made the choice to accept far less than He deserved to give us far more than we deserve:

- He gave up a throne for a manger (and a cross).
- He gave up majestic splendor for suffering and shame.

- He laid aside His rights as the Son and took the role of a servant.

- He put aside the garments of glory and took upon himself the flesh of humanity.

The first measure of how much Christ loves us is found in what He was willing to leave behind to come to our rescue—by coming to the earth to be one of us. Before we can begin to understand what He did when He got here, we must see what He left behind to become the Servant-model we need.

Longtime minister of London's Westminster Chapel, D. Martin Lloyd-Jones, said of Philippians 2:6–11, "I am sure we will all agree that this entire passage is one of the most magnificent in the whole Bible!"[2] Why? Because in it we learn of the very heart and mind that drove Christ—God become man for us. This is what Paul was expressing in 1 Timothy 3:16:

By common confession, great is the mystery of godliness: He who was revealed in the flesh, was vindicated in the Spirit, seen by angels, proclaimed among the nations, believed on in the world, taken up in glory.

Like Emily Elliott, Paul urges us to look beyond the manger to see what Jesus set aside to be our Savior. They are both encouraging us to see what Jesus left behind to come to our rescue.

The God Who Empties Himself (Philippians 2:7)

Paul makes one more dramatic assertion about the sacrificial, servant mind-set of the Christ who came, and we need to see it in its full context. He wrote:

> Have this attitude in yourselves which was also in Christ Jesus, who, although He existed in the form of God, did not regard equality with God a thing to be grasped, but emptied Himself, taking the form of a bond-servant, and being made in the likeness of men. (Philippians 2:5–7)

Here we land on the concept of *kenosis*, which was mentioned earlier. It is found in the word *emptied* (Greek *kenoo*; v. 7). When we think of "emptying," we think of "lessening," like emptying a jug of milk. The terms here are a bit more nuanced. The word *kenosis* doesn't speak as much of a "pouring out" as it does a "setting aside."

What might this look like? Stories are told about King James V of Scotland who, recognizing the distance that separated him from his subjects, would from time to time set aside his royal robes, throne, privileges, and status to dress in the clothes of a commoner and wander among the people. His goal? To better understand life outside the castle and to live that life for a time among the people. This willful act of humility allowed the king to step into a world very different from the one his status deserved.

In a far more profound way, Jesus not only stepped away from His heavenly place and privilege but He also came to this earth—to this world with its ugliness and struggles and pain. In this daring demonstration of true humility, we find the second measure of His great love for us. It adds to what He left behind by describing where He came and what He experienced here.

Emily Steele Elliott's hymn captures this idea as well, as the second verse states:

> Heaven's arches rang when the angels sang,
> Proclaiming Thy royal degree;
> But of lowly birth didst Thou come to earth,
> And in great humility.

Once again, this great hymn peeks into the mystery of the incarnation. And it was not just the lowly birth that validated it—it was also the life He entered into in order to bring us to himself. Again, see how Paul echoes this idea, saying that Jesus "emptied Himself, taking the form of a bond-servant, and being made in the likeness of men" (Philippians 2:7).

Three big ideas ring forth from Philippians 2:7, and all of them speak to the humility of God the Son:

- **Emptied himself.** Jesus became a human person, and without ceasing to be God, He laid aside the privileges of being equal with God in order to redeem us. He possessed full deity—but He didn't cling to it. What does it mean? He laid aside His self-will in order to be a servant and die.

- **Form of a slave.** This means he took on (or added to His divine essence) the exact essence and nature of a servant. Even though He was equal to the Father, He willingly became a slave. This speaks of the extreme humility of Christ— and what an example of self-sacrifice that is!

- **Likeness of men.** The key here is the word *likeness*. It is different from *form* (vv. 6–7), but it is the perfect word to describe the God-man. It carries the idea of strong similarity while leaving room for recognizable differences. He was fully human, yet different from all other human beings because He was God and without sin.

Consider what it meant for God the Son to become "Immanuel" (God with us). Think of what He gave up for you and me: "For you know the grace of our Lord Jesus Christ, that though He was rich, yet for your sake He became poor, so that you through His poverty might become rich" (2 Corinthians 8:9).

Many times, people who don't even know Jesus extol His greatness—yet they may overlook the very realities that made Him truly great. In the incarnation He did the following remarkable things:

He accepted a servant's place;
He entered a sinful world;
He adopted a selfless attitude.

The Mind of Christ

For followers of Christ, this speaks deeply to our own attitudes toward life. In Romans 8:29, we find the ultimate goal of our rescue clearly stated: "For those whom

He foreknew, He also predestined to become conformed to the image of His Son, so that He would be the firstborn among many brethren."

We have been rescued to be made like Jesus. With that in view, remember that Paul launched into his very different and highly theological telling of the Christmas story with a similar challenge, saying: "Have this attitude [mind-set] in yourselves which was also in Christ Jesus" (Philippians 2:5).

When we understand who Christ is, what He left, and how He came, Christ's mind-set is clearly one of servanthood and self-sacrifice—long before He took a basin and towel to wash the disciples' feet, and long before He went to the cross, allowing himself to be sacrificed as the Lamb of God who came to take away the sins of the world (John 1:29). Christ's sacrifice and servant's heart are first seen in eternity past as He chose to set aside His rights and privileges as God to come in the essence of a slave.

How could that mind-set be expressed in our lives? Our hearts? Our relationships? Our attitudes? This should be our greatest desire and longing: that our God, by His Spirit, would build into us this mind-set. The mind-set of servanthood. The mind-set of self-sacrifice. The mind-set of the Christ who came.

This is the challenge that rings out from the old gospel chorus that prays:

> To be like Jesus,
> To be like Jesus!
> All I ask—to be like Him.
> All through life's journey
> From earth to glory—
> All I ask—to be like Him.

2

His Relationship with the Father

*Because Jesus was eternally equal
with the Father,
the Father and Son shared
everything perfectly.*

When I was a boy, one program on television revolutionized the craft of storytelling: *The Twilight Zone*. Rather than telling linear stories with a logical trajectory and predictable, usually happy, endings (aside from the occasional surprise twist at the end), this show surprised and delighted viewers with its outside-the-box approach. Often thought of as a science fiction program, *The Twilight Zone* was more psychologically rooted, approaching the challenge of storytelling from a variety of different angles. Rod Serling, the genius behind *The Twilight Zone*, was a master of both the ironic and the unexpected. As a result, the viewer was forced to ponder possibilities and imagine the unimaginable—all the while being made to feel just ever-so-slightly off-balance.

For me, this was a mind-bending proposition. This kind of counterintuitive, countercultural approach shaped the way I came to view other things as well—with the impossible no longer unthinkable and with the what-ifs now in play. I approached the gap between what could or could not be, at least at a psychological level, no longer with outrageous disbelief, but with quiet wondering.

This may seem like an odd way to begin a chapter on the relationship of God the Father and God the Son in eternity past, but in a sense it is also precisely the point. How do we begin to imagine that which is utterly beyond us? Even with some biblical information to support our ponderings, it is difficult to grasp what heaven will be like in eternity future—let alone what it was like in eternity past. As Bart Millard put it in MercyMe's blockbuster song: "I can only imagine."

With a clear sense of reverence and mystery, ancient hymnwriter Prudentius (AD 348–413) attempted to plumb those depths, writing:

> Born of God the Father's bosom,
>   Ere the worlds began to be,
> Omega and Alpha named,
>   He the first the ending He
> Of all things that are or have been,
>   Or that time to come shall see,
>   Ever and for evermore.

Clearly, this is a challenging subject. It is a gargantuan task to pull back the veil of eternity and picture the wonder of the scene. However, it is a vital part of our journey into the Christmas backstory.

Why? In order to comprehend the majesty of the gift of Christ to us, we must understand the eternal depth with which the Father loved the Son. And that powerful love is at the heart of our rescue as well.

So, where do we begin this journey into the unimaginable? We are given an intimate glimpse of the relationship between the first and second persons of the Godhead in Jesus's own words. We begin with Jesus's longest recorded prayer in the Scriptures—His prayer recorded in John 17. We'll look at Jesus's shared glory, His shared love, and His shared mission.

A Moment of Reflection

As a student in Bible college, I took a course called hermeneutics. This is not to be confused with its cousin, homiletics, which deals with the preparation and delivery of sermons. Rather, hermeneutics deals with the science and art of interpreting the Scriptures. Few subjects are more important than reading Scripture clearly and accurately, so I approached this course with intensity, wanting the best opportunity possible to "rightly divide the word of truth" (see 2 Timothy 2:15 NKJV).

Given such a lofty goal, I expected scholarly formulas and academic rigor to be at the heart of handling Scripture—and believe me, those things did factor into the process. But imagine my surprise when in the early days of the semester the prof told us that the majority of sound interpretation is found in exploring, understanding, and honoring the context of the passage at hand. I discovered that nothing will drive our understanding more significantly than the layers of context that surround the text itself—and that is absolutely true of Jesus's prayer in John 17.

Before we consider how this prayer informs our understanding of the eternal relationship between Father and Son, we must see it in its context—the great linchpin between the events of the upper room (John 13–16) and the events of Jesus's passion (John 18–20).

In the upper room, we find Jesus's final teaching session with His disciples. It is a time filled with example (washing their feet), worship (celebration of Passover), betrayal (Judas leaves), warning (Peter's boasts confronted), instruction (anticipating the coming of the Holy Spirit), and preparation for the dark night of the soul awaiting these men. And they are not ready for what lies ahead. When the events of Christ's suffering and sacrifice begin to unfold in the garden of Gethsemane, they will scatter in fear—abandoning the Christ and hiding in darkness.

This critical moment motivates a prayer—and it is a remarkable prayer, to say the least. In the prayer, Jesus prays for them at this most delicate moment, and He prays for us and the life we would experience in Him. His concerns for them (and us) in the midst of His anticipation of the suffering before Him are nothing short of stunning.

But that was not all He prayed about. Woven throughout His words of mission and ministry, dangers and disciples, Jesus also reflects on His relationship with His Father—not just in that moment of time but also in eternity past. As much as anything else, it was a relationship marked by what they shared.

One other thought. In the Old Testament, the writers used literary devices to communicate their ideas to their generation, particularly in their poetry and prayers. Although John was writing in Greek, his context and thinking were profoundly Jewish, so he would have been fully aware of and familiar with these devices—as would Jesus. Modern scholars refer to one such device as a *chiasm*, a term based on the Greek letter *chi*, or X. The ideas mirror one another with the main point being in the center of the X. While I can't prove that Jesus's prayer is technically a chiasm, it without question functions as a chiasm as the relationship of Father and Son is celebrated. Notice how these thoughts play out.

1. Shared Mission (17:3)
   2. Shared Glory (17:5)
      3. Shared Love (17:23–24)
   2a. Shared Knowledge/Glory (17:25)
1a. Shared Mission (17:26)

As the ideas build to and from the center, the main idea becomes clear. While it is eternally relevant that the Father and Son have a shared glory, and it is eternally important for *us* that the Father and Son have a shared mission, the most significant idea is at the center—the shared love of the Father and Son (reinforced in verses 23, 24, and 26).

Shared Glory

"Now, Father, glorify Me together with Yourself, with *the glory which I had with You* before the world was." (John 17:5; emphasis mine)

"O righteous Father, although *the world has not known You*, yet I have known You; and these have known that You sent Me." (John 17:25; emphasis mine)

Some years ago, a movie rooted in history celebrated the first African-American units to serve in the United

States Army—and it was during the Civil War. The film was entitled *Glory*, and it was brilliant storytelling. But in the end, almost all the key characters died. Glory in death by combat?

Many times in sports we see an athlete attempt the absurd—for example, an unbelievable catch by a center fielder with his outstretched arm over the wall as he attempts to pull a home run back into the field of play. It's called "going for glory." Glory by fame and acclaim?

The concept of *glory* as it is used in our culture can be a little murky. And that is true within the family of faith as well. It seems that *glory* is one of those words in the Christian vocabulary (like *holy*, *righteousness*, or *judgment*) that is badly misunderstood and as a result is regularly misapplied. So then, what is glory?

In Hebrew, the language of most of the Old Testament, the word we translate as *glory* is the term *kabod*. Its New Testament parallel, *doxa*, is the root of our word *doxology* (a doxology is a declaration [logos] of the glory [doxa] of God). But what *is* that glory? Biblical scholar Dr. Kenneth Bailey made an important clarification as he dealt with 1 Corinthians 1 in his book *Paul Through Mediterranean Eyes*, in which he wrote:

> The Greek word *doxa* (glory) is the Hebrew word *kabod* (weight). In Middle Eastern culture, a "weighty" person (*rajul thaqil*) has to do with wisdom, balance, stability, reliability, sound judgment, patience, impartiality, nobility and the like. Latin has preserved these ideas and attached them to the word *gravitas*. Glory has to do with *gravitas*! Every family, community and church desperately wants and needs such a person to guide them, comfort them and help them solve their problems. God's plan for all ages has to do with the cross and with the emergence on the other side of the cross of men and women who embody these qualities. Indeed glory (*gravitas*), for those who love God, flows from the cross of "the Lord of glory."[1]

This is critical as we seek to understand the eternal relationship of the Father and the Son. In Bailey's words, the understanding of a first-century Jew (which was the case of both Jesus, who spoke these words, and John, who recorded them) meant that this *gravitas* described a person who pictured "wisdom, balance, stability, reliability, sound judgment, patience, impartiality, nobility." Put another way, a *kabod* person was someone who was a person of substance in the best and most important ways.

We might believe that about the eternal Father, but what about the Son? Not only does Jesus here claim that this was a divine *gravitas* He had shared with the Father from all eternity past, but John also affirms that human beings witnessed the evidence of that fact in Jesus, who came from heaven to be Immanuel, or "God with us." John wrote: "And the Word became flesh, and dwelt among us, and we saw His glory, glory as of the only begotten from the Father, full of grace and truth" (John 1:14).

What John declared, Jesus affirmed as He prayed to His Father in John 17: "Father, glorify Me together with Yourself, with the glory which I had with You before the world was" (v. 5). The gravitas that is true only of God was shared by the Christ before the world began. How is that glory characterized? By grace and truth that are substantial, significant, and wise. This is grace and truth that are part of the absolute essence of who God is. These are not just theoretical ideas.

How is that expressed in relationship? In the perfect, shared knowledge of Father and Son (John 17:25). We cannot really know God in His glory apart from it being revealed to us in Jesus, as Moses learned in the Old Testament. While on the mountain of God receiving the law for the fledgling nation of Israel, Moses made a shocking request. He said to God, "Show me Your glory" (Exodus 33:18). God's response?

He said, "I Myself will make all My goodness pass before you, and will proclaim the name of the LORD before you; and I will be gracious to whom I will be gracious, and will show compassion on whom I will show compassion." But He said, "You cannot see My face, for no man can see Me and live!" (Exodus 33:19–20)

What Moses longed to see can only be experienced through Jesus, the coming of God to us, who displayed that shared glory so completely that Paul would write: "For God, who said, 'Light shall shine out of darkness,' is the One who has shone in our hearts to give the Light of the knowledge of the glory of God in the face of Christ" (2 Corinthians 4:6).

The light of God's glory—unbearable to the eyes of broken human beings—has been made available to us in Christ. He was God in human flesh, and He had shared that glory with the Father since a past forever. Now *that* is gravitas, and we will revisit it when we consider Jesus's preparations for the cross.

Shared Love

The Father and the Son have a shared love that is independent of creation, independent of humanity, independent of everything. Placed strategically at the crux of the chiasm (X), what we need to learn most from Jesus's prayer is the power of the love of the Father and the Son. From all eternity past, there was never a moment without perfect, selfless love expressed between them.

This is a pretty difficult (impossible perhaps?) idea to grasp. We tend to think of love within the realm of time and experience. I remember the first time I saw Marlene. Although I would not describe the moment as "love at first sight," there was something remarkable that I sensed was going to rock my world. I remember that moment—everything about it—and it was something of a watershed event. Life became divided into two distinct experiences—before I met Marlene and after I met Marlene.

When our children were born, there was a tangible, palpable sense of love for those little ones from the moment of their birth. There was no verbal communication (aside from the occasional wail), no shared experience. There were none of the things that usually contribute to the development of relational love. Nevertheless, those unmistakable and indescribable moments of real, powerful love are locked into a moment in time—and have endured ever since.

Because we live our lives encased in time, the concept of a relationship that had no beginning and will have no ending is a little hard to process. Nevertheless, once again, the Scriptures pull back the curtain and give us a quick glimpse into the eternal past. Jesus, in prayer with His Father, celebrates a love of immeasurable value. It is a love that is timeless because it existed before time existed.

> I in them and You in Me, that they may be perfected in unity, so that the world may know that You sent Me, and loved them, *even as You have*

loved Me. Father, I desire that they also, whom
You have given Me, be with Me where I am, so
that they may see My glory which You have given
Me, for *You loved Me* before the foundation of the
world. (John 17:23–24; emphasis added)

This love contributes to what makes the incarnation (God coming in human flesh) so mindboggling.
It was not just that Jesus stepped from heaven to earth.
It wasn't just that He left perfection to embrace imperfection. He stepped out of that perfect relationship of
love to come here and give hope to a world in need of
relationship with God. His coming would challenge
all of our relationships as well.

Why? Because, in our brokenness, our relationships
would be marked by self-interest instead of selfless
concern for others. Only in the Christ could we see
what real love looks like. Only in Him could the love
that was lost by our rebellion be restored. In *The Yale
Anchor Bible*, Raymond Brown gives us a sense of the
sweeping grandeur of this love between Father and
Son—a love that has been extended to us!

The standard of comparison is breathtaking but
logical. . . . God loves these children as He loves

His Son. It would seem that love is incapable of existing in various degrees. If love is "selfless concern in action on behalf of the other," then God's love is not parceled out in degrees, depending on the worth or condition of the one loved.[2]

The result? The selfless concern shared in that perfect relationship reaches beyond that perfection to all of the imperfection and brokenness that is humanity. The result of that shared love is mission—a mission that would be resolved by Jesus's coming.

Shared Mission

"This is eternal life, that they may know You, the only true God, and Jesus Christ *whom You have sent.*" (John 17:3; emphasis added)

"*I have made Your name known* to them, and will make it known, so that the love with which You loved Me may be in them, and I in them." (John 17:26; emphasis added)

Here Jesus reveals two different perspectives on His divine mission. The first is that He was sent by the Father with a long-term purpose. The second is that

He also had a short-term goal. As we saw earlier, the beloved apostle John gives a glimpse into that short-term goal: "No one has seen God at any time; the only begotten God who is in the bosom of the Father, He has explained Him" (John 1:18).

This was the short-term mission, and it related to Jesus and His twelve disciples. He had not only assembled them and taught them, and He had not only modeled servanthood and practiced compassion, but He had also done exactly what John 1:18 promised. He had explained the Father to them by showing them, in human flesh, what the Father is truly like. This was the immediate mission, and as the disciples went forward telling of the Christ, it was a message of how Jesus had revealed the heart of His Father. Again, the magnitude of this must not be underestimated. The invisible God sent His Son in visible form so we could understand Him. Amazing!

But the mission went beyond that short-term influence. It ended in an eternal solution to the human problem. In John 17:3, Jesus says that eternal life is found in knowing the Father—but how? How could we know Him when our sin has so distanced us from Him? As the Old Testament prophet Isaiah wrote:

"But your iniquities have made a separation between you and your God, and your sins have hidden His face from you so that He does not hear" (Isaiah 59:2).

We were separated from God, and the gap could never be bridged from our side of the chasm. So in eternity past the Father and the Son agreed together that when creation took place, when people were given choice, and when rebellion occurred, the bridge would be built from the side of the Godhead. And Jesus would build that bridge with His cross.

Yet while that cross would be the ultimate demonstration of God's love for us (Romans 5:8), that redemptive mission would also be the perfect expression of the mutual love between the Father and the Son. Jesus underlined that important idea in His teaching on the "Good Shepherd" in John 10 when He said, "For this reason the Father loves Me, because I lay down My life so that I may take it again" (v. 17).

Dr. Gary Burge, writing in *The Bible Knowledge Background Commentary: John's Gospel*, pulls this together beautifully: "[In] Jesus' voluntary death therefore is a hallmark of his union with the Father's will and an expression of the love they share together."[3] In the eternal shared relationship of Father and Son, we see love and mission intertwined. For us. For our rescue.

The eternal glory of God anticipated our brokenness with gravitas—a substantial, weighty response—and the mission for our rescue was birthed of their love for one another. We will examine this powerful rescue mission more fully in the next chapter, but it can never be divorced from all that the Father and Son shared before the world was created. The glory, love, and mission of the Father and the Son (implemented by the Holy Spirit) are at the very heart of the cross.

Shared with Us

Throughout the two millennia since Jesus walked the earth, His followers have often turned to music to try to get a handle on the profoundly challenging issues of eternity, divine love, and perfect compassion. Whether it is "O Sacred Head Now Wounded," which scrutinizes the cross; or "Be Thou My Vision," which wrestles with God's abiding care for His children, we have sought music that could help us grasp things that are clearly beyond our finite understanding.

In 1726 hymnwriter Nicolaus von Zinzendorf wrestled with the same eternal issues we have been considering and sought to capture them in the lyrics of his hymn "Eternal Depth of Love Divine."

> Eternal depth of love divine,
> In Jesus, God with us, displayed;
> How brightly Thy beaming glories shine!
> How wide Thy healing streams are spread!
>
> With whom dost Thou delight to dwell?
> Sinners, a vile and thankless race!
> O God, what tongue aright can tell
> How vast Thy love, how great Thy grace!
>
> To Thy sure love, Thy tender care,
> Our flesh, soul, spirit, we resign;
> O, fix Thy sacred presence there,
> And seal the abode for ever Thine!

As is often the case with words of such weight, we struggle with the language and style intended for the ears of a different generation. What we do know is this: the Father and the Son, who shared perfect glory and perfect love, also shared a powerful mission to extend that love to us. In Jesus, the glory and love of the Father come to our rescue. And *that* we can understand. It is as simple as:

> Jesus loves me this I know
> For the Bible tells me so.

We'll explore that mission from the perspective of eternity past next.

3

His Preparation
for the Cross

*God prepared the way for our rescue
by determining that His Son
would go to the cross for us—
before the world was even created.*

At the beginning of the 2015–2016 English Premier
League football (soccer) season, Leicester City (the
Foxes) were fortunate to still be in the league. The
previous season had been a disaster, and they had
almost been relegated, or dropped out of the league
to the next-lower division. This is an unusual concept
for many Americans to grasp, but it would be something like the Detroit Tigers having such a bad season

in Major League Baseball that the entire organization would be sent down to play the next year in the Triple-A level, with another Triple-A minor league team coming into the majors to take their place. That is the devastation of relegation in English football.

Barely avoiding relegation, the Foxes were considered 5,000 to 1 odds to win the league. Yet with a precocious set of players and an outside-the-box manager, they shocked the football world by winning the toughest league on the planet. As they marched toward the title, pundits and analysts began to refer to them as a "team of destiny"—and that destiny was fulfilled on May 2, 2016, as they lifted the Premier League trophy and celebrated an unlikely championship. Glorious destiny!

In the United States of America in the 1800s, people came to believe in the doctrine of Manifest Destiny. This term was first used in 1845 by a journalist named John L. Sullivan to describe an intentional approach to the growth of the republic. Manifest Destiny held that there was an inherent right for the fledgling nation to spread across North America and build a nation that would stretch from sea to shining sea. While the subsequent growth of the American nation built one of the richest and most powerful countries the world has ever seen, it carried with it a dark side—the intentional near-genocide of Native American tribes and a sweeping disregard for the land itself. Manifest Destiny.

William Shakespeare provided his own take on destiny in arguably his greatest work, *Romeo and Juliet*. Here, the star-crossed (that is, negatively destined or predetermined) young lovers from rival families (Capulet and Montague) are drawn irresistibly to one another in their love, its secret consummation, and their ultimate preference to take their lives rather than be forced to live out their families' mutual hatred and anger. In the closing scene, Prince Escalus mourns the loss of these two young people—and the feud that seemed to drive them to an unwanted end. Tragic destiny.

What is *destiny*? It is the sense that something—a result, outcome, or event—is inevitable because it has somehow been predetermined. Some will talk of destiny by using the word *fate*, but it is the same idea. (It is interesting to notice how many people who hold to fate or destiny have nothing to identify as the first cause behind the expected result. If there is no one to predetermine things, how can we think of such a thing as destiny or fate?)

As such, it is both ironic and mysterious that the eternal Christ, who, as we have seen, was and is and forevermore will be alive, entered this world with a destiny that pointed beyond His life to His death. Without in any way diminishing the amazing realities of His life, His was a destiny that was birthed in the wisdom of God in eternity past, accepted by the Son, and completed in this world. More than any other person ever to walk this planet, He was born to die.

This destiny is rooted in one of the most mysterious concepts in the Scriptures. In eternity past, no created thing yet existed, rebellion had not happened, and there had been no experience of death. Yet the Son was destined to die. How could this be?

Quite candidly, we have far more questions than we do answers. Some theologians speak of these mysteries in terms of "decrees." In these determined decisions, God (Father, Son, Spirit) decreed that the universe would be brought into being and that the crown of that creation would be human beings, made in the image of God. But in order for humans to be in the image of

God, they needed to have a will—and the free exercise of that will. So God also decreed that man and woman would have choice—knowing that we would rebel against Him and His perfect love.

Before the creation ever occurred and before the "fall" ever took place (see Genesis 3:1–15), God also decreed that He would rescue that rebellious creation by sending His Son to the world to suffer death for everyone (Hebrews 2:9). Therefore, before the world began, it was determined that Jesus's destiny would be to die for the sins of the world.

Is that exactly how it all happened? The Scriptures don't tell us. But they do tell us enough to let us know that the Father's eternal purposes included the destiny of the cross for God the Son. Those Scriptures won't unlock every door of understanding or unravel every mystery, but the voices those Scriptures represent can help us see how deeply, and eternally, we are loved by our God.

We'll see these voices in reverse chronological order, starting with Paul.

The Voice of Paul

I love Paul. I love his brilliance, his devotion to Christ, his intentional, purposeful living. I love so many things about the apostle Paul.

But I also love the fact that Paul had a quirky side. He was not above using sarcasm in writing to the Corinthians (2 Corinthians 11:19), he struggled sometimes to remember personal details from his own life (1 Corinthians 1), and, in writing to the Philippian church, he told them to focus on "one thing"—and then listed *three* things (Philippians 3:13–14). Indeed, Paul was quirky.

In a different expression of his quirkiness, Paul, when trying to wrestle with the eternal mystery of the cross, wrote what, in the Greek, is one of the longest sentences in the Bible—twelve verses long! We see it in Ephesians 1:

> Blessed be the God and Father of our Lord Jesus Christ, who has blessed us with every spiritual blessing in the heavenly places in Christ, just as He chose us in Him before the foundation of the world, that we would be holy and blameless before Him. In love He predestined us to adoption as

sons through Jesus Christ to Himself, according to the kind intention of His will, to the praise of the glory of His grace, which He freely bestowed on us in the Beloved. In Him we have redemption through His blood, the forgiveness of our trespasses, according to the riches of His grace which He lavished on us. In all wisdom and insight He made known to us the mystery of His will, according to His kind intention which He purposed in Him with a view to an administration suitable to the fullness of the times, that is, the summing up of all things in Christ, things in the heavens and things on the earth. In Him also we have obtained an inheritance, having been predestined according to His purpose who works all things after the counsel of His will, to the end that we who were the first to hope in Christ would be to the praise of His glory. In Him, you also, after listening to the message of truth, the gospel of your salvation—having also believed, you were sealed in Him with the Holy Spirit of promise, who is given as a pledge of our inheritance, with a view to the redemption of God's own possession, to the praise of His glory. (Ephesians 1:3–14)

Without dealing with all of the complexities of this demanding text, we can examine the themes that rise to the surface—themes that can inform the eternal nature of the gospel plan.

First, Paul says that we were chosen "in Him," meaning Jesus, before the foundation of the world (v. 4). The only way that can be true is if the redemptive plan for us was established in Him before the foundation of the world. This important idea is reinforced in verses 5 through 7 where we see our adoption into God's family directly linked to our "redemption through His blood"—a reminder of the cost of our rescue on the cross. How was this accomplished? It was accomplished "according to His purpose who works all things after the counsel of His will" (v. 11).

Once again, we have in view the purpose and counsel that had been established before the world began. Paul's highly theological view of the cross is that everything Jesus accomplished there in us, for us, and through us was all part of the plan. It was the destiny Christ had come to fulfill—and the results of that choice in the eternal past reach forward into eternity yet to come. To that end John wrote, "We have seen and testify that the Father has sent the Son to be the Savior of the world" (1 John 4:14).

In Philippians 2 (which we saw in part in chapter 1), Paul added his own postscript to this dramatic turn by saying, "Being found in appearance as a man, He humbled Himself by becoming obedient to the point of death, even death on a cross" (v. 8).

The Father sent, and the Son came. The plan of the ages took human form as the Word became flesh (John 1:14). The destiny of the Christ saw Him implementing that plan all the way to death on a cross. Perhaps this lengthy, complex gathering of ideas (Ephesians 1:3–14) exists because Paul found it so difficult to capture in human words the wonder of this divine plan.

The Voice of Peter

When I was a boy, I saw the film *The Greatest Story Ever Told*—a cinematic telling of the life of Christ. The film boasted an all-star cast that included Charlton Heston as John the Baptist, David McCallum as Judas Iscariot, John Wayne as the centurion at the cross, and Max Von Sydow as Jesus. The film was at times fanciful and at other times biblical, but it was one filmmaker's attempt to tell that great story.

When Dr. M. R. DeHaan founded a new Bible-teaching radio ministry in 1938—a ministry that would become Our Daily Bread Ministries—he made a strategic choice for the theme music for that radio program. He chose "Tell Me the Story of Jesus," which declares:

> Tell me the story of Jesus,
> Write on my heart every word;
> Tell me the story most precious,
> Sweetest that ever was heard.

At the end of the day, the message of the cross is a story. And although we don't often think of it this way, on the day of Pentecost Peter became the first person to clearly tell that story. For us it is an old, old story, but for Peter, as recorded in Acts 2, it was a brand-new story.

The greatest story ever told.

Just seven weeks after the events of the cross and the resurrection of Jesus, and just ten days after Jesus ascended to heaven, Peter revealed that there was more to the story. There was a backstory to the greatest of all stories. A story about eternal destiny. He said:

> Men of Israel, listen to these words: Jesus the Nazarene, a man attested to you by God with miracles and wonders and signs which God performed through Him in your midst, just as you yourselves know—this Man, delivered over by the predetermined plan and foreknowledge of God, you nailed to a cross by the hands of godless men and put Him to death. (Acts 2:22–23)

This statement forms the core of Peter's sermon, and it is populated by four critical statements that build on one another:

1. Jesus was a living person who did wonderful things.

2. These miraculous deeds were evidence of God working through Him.

3. This Man was delivered to crucifixion by God from eternity past.

4. Human beings still bear responsibility for their actions.

For our purposes, it is the third statement that jumps to the front of the line. Notice that Jesus was "delivered over by the predetermined plan and foreknowledge of God" to the cross (v. 23). Here Peter is stating what Paul would later write in Ephesians 1: the cross was undeniably Jesus's eternally determined destiny. Theology professor Stanley Toussaint wrote:

> The point of this verse is clear: the Crucifixion was no accident. It was in **God's set purpose** (*boulē*, "plan") and was God's determined will, not merely His inclination. It was a divine necessity (cf. 4:28).[1]

In *The Expositor's Bible Commentary*, R. N. Longenecker wrote:

> The death of Jesus is presented as resulting from the interplay of divine necessity and human freedom. Nowhere in the NT is the paradox of a Christian understanding of history put more sharply than in this earliest proclamation of the death of Jesus the Messiah: God's purpose and foreknowledge stand as the necessary factors behind whatever happens; yet whatever happens occurs through the instrumentality of wicked men

expressing their own human freedom. It is a paradox without ready solution. To deny it, however, is to go counter to the plain teaching of Scripture (both OT and NT) and to ignore the testimony of personal experience.[2]

In part, this was why the Jewish religious leaders failed to recognize Jesus as their Messiah. They could not imagine a crucified Christ. Yet, while this story is filled with both mystery and divine purpose, that was the destiny of the Christ. The cross and the resurrection, ultimately, as Peter confirmed at Pentecost, validated Jesus as the Son and the Savior: "But God raised Him up again, putting an end to the agony of death, since it was impossible for Him to be held in its power" (Acts 2:24).

The Voice of Jesus

Whether in the now-ancient TV show *Mission: Impossible* or in the run of recent movies of the same name, one of popular entertainment's most familiar lines must be, "Your mission, should you choose to accept it . . ." First uttered to Dan Briggs, the original leader of the Impossible Mission Force, this *Mission: Impossible* challenge would also be delivered to Jim Phelps and, more recently, Ethan Hunt. The words, however, leave open the door of refusal. They offer an option. A Plan B. A way out. Apparently, the mission could be turned down if the leader would so choose.

The mission of rescue to which the Father called the Son in eternity past was one from which the Christ would never shrink. The way out was never an option—even in Gethsemane when Jesus concluded His three seasons of prayer by saying to His Father, "yet not My will, but Yours be done" (Luke 22:42).

From Jesus's earliest recorded words, He was on mission. Even as a twelve-year-old child, He was found in the temple confounding the scholars. His reason for being there? "Why is it that you were looking for Me? Did you not know that I had to be in My Father's house?" (Luke 2:49). From that moment forward, Jesus was moving irrevocably on a predetermined path—the path that would lead to the cross.

As the week of His passion arrived, just days before going to the cross, Jesus was teaching in the temple when two of His disciples, Andrew and Philip, arrived with a request. A group of gentile "God-fearers" (possibly proselytes, or converts, to Judaism) had requested a meeting with the Teacher (John 12:22–23). Honestly, at first blush, Jesus's response seems a bit odd—but in fact it was both direct and profound.

> "Now My soul has become troubled; and what shall I say, 'Father, save Me from this hour'? But for this purpose I came to this hour. Father, glorify Your name." Then a voice came out of heaven: "I have both glorified it, and will glorify it again." So the crowd of people who stood by and heard it were saying that it had thundered; others were saying, "An angel has spoken to Him." Jesus answered and said, "This voice has not come for My sake, but for your sakes. Now judgment is upon this world; now the ruler of this world will be cast out. And I, if I am lifted up from the earth, will draw all men to Myself." But He was saying this to indicate the kind of death by which He was to die. (John 12:27–33)

Notice the bookends of this text:

- But for this purpose I came to this hour.
- He was saying this to indicate the kind of death by which He was to die.

In Jesus's heart and mind, there was never any question why He had been sent to this earth. We often hear people quote this text, saying that they want to "lift Jesus up in worship so He can draw all men to himself," but that is not what is in view. He had come into the world and to that very hour for the purpose of bearing the sins of the world by being lifted up on the cross (1 Peter 2:24).

In that self-sacrificial act, Jesus not only fulfilled His destiny—established in eternity past—but He also made a way back to God for us. And in doing that, He made the one truly undeniable statement in all of history about the Father's love.

Often, when we are struggling, suffering, confused, or despairing, we wrestle with doubts about the true nature of the heart of God. We can wonder, "Does God love me? If God loved me, why would this be happening to me?" And in that moment of desperation, there is one answer. An eternal answer. A complete proof of God's love.

The cross.

As Paul wrote: "But God demonstrates His own love toward us, in that while we were yet sinners, Christ died for us" (Romans 5:8).

The legitimacy of God's love is not measured by the circumstances I face—good, bad, or indifferent. The legitimacy of God's love is proven by the Christ and His cross. The wonder of that is magnified exponentially when we remember that before the world was ever created God had determined to pay this price for our rebellion before we even rebelled. No wonder Charles Wesley, seeking just the right words, expressed with awe:

> Amazing love! How can it be,
> That Thou, my God, shouldst die for me?

Indeed.

Always the Only Plan

Like many of my generation, I grew up on the Authorized Version of the Bible, most widely known as the King James Version (KJV). The rich (though often challenging) Elizabethan English gave a sense of awe and dignity to what I read. As newer versions of the Scriptures have overtaken the KJV, scholars are convinced that today's Bible translations are more accurate than the Authorized Version, yet perhaps lacking its beauty. Nevertheless, I grew up with the King James and most of the Scripture I have memorized over the years comes from that translation.

One of my favorite verses in the KJV is stated in such a way that makes the eternal purposes of God unmistakable. Undeniable. There was only ever going to be one plan—one destiny—for the Christ who would come. It is John the beloved apostle, who records it for us: "And all that dwell upon the earth shall worship [the beast], whose names are not written in the book of life of the Lamb slain from the foundation of the world" (Revelation 13:8).

Here, we see both ends of that destiny. In eternity past, the destiny pointed to the cross and Jesus's sacrifice for the sins of the world. Now, in the aftermath of the cross and resurrection, the second destiny begins to take form—anticipating the time to come when the names of many would be written in the Lamb's Book of Life.

Perhaps that is why the writer of Hebrews said that Jesus, "for the joy set before Him endured the cross, despising the shame, and has sat down at the right hand of the throne of God" (12:2). For the joy! A joy that He saw from eternity past, to a moment in history on a cross of suffering, to an eternity of celebration. It is that celebration that we anticipate every time we sing Matthew Bridges' words:

> Crown Him with many crowns,
> The Lamb upon His throne;
> Hark! How the heav'nly anthem drowns
> All music but its own!
> Awake, my soul and sing
> Of Him Who died for thee,
> And hail Him as thy matchless King
> Through all eternity.

4

His Role as Creator

Christ was the primary member of the Trinity
at work in the creation of the universe.

Are you a creative person? I'm not. I'm just not that clever. But my friend, the late Steve Bly, was uber-creative. Steve was a husband, father, pastor, town mayor, and writer; but, especially, Steve was a cowboy. While comfortable writing books about Christian living and biblical theology, Steve also had a special knack for writing Christian Western fiction. He would continually spin characters and stories out of his head that were, at the same time, incredible and fully believable.

One of Steve's fun things to do was to write his friends into his books—and I was one of them.

Characterized as an old-school Western lawman pursuing justice, "Old Bill Crowder" found a mention in one of his novels in the Tap Andrews series. When I jokingly asked him about that mention, Steve spun a tantalizing tale of Old Bill pursuing outlaws into a canyon where he was trapped and eventually gunned down by the desperadoes in a hail of bullets, taking a handful of bad guys with him. The ease and winsomeness with which Steve could create the story out of thin air amazed me. Creative talent usually does.

Most of the time, however, when we talk about creativity, we are actually talking about *making*, not *creating*. Making is taking materials available—paint and canvas for an artist, notes and instruments for a musician, granite or marble for a sculptor, processors and wires for a techno-wizard—and using them to make something else. And while that takes great creativity, it is not true creation. True creation is taking *nothing* and making something out of it. Theologians refer to this as "creation ex nihilo," or "creation out of nothing."

This is the massive difference between songwriting, for example, and what we are given in Genesis 1. When the Bible opens with the words, "In the beginning God created," it is the most astounding statement on the power and person of God that we could ever imagine. When we gaze out over an ocean, ponder a starry night sky, investigate the microbiology of an utterly unseen world, or fly over the North Pole, it should take our breath away. It should fill us with awe and wonder that our God is so powerful that everything we see was created out of raw materials that did not previously exist.

As a very young follower of Christ, I had the privilege of hearing the great African-American preacher Shadrach Meshach Lockridge preach on creation. His clever and dramatic presentation began something like this: "Long, long time ago, way back when there was nothing there but God, God reached out and grabbed a big handful of nothing and declared, 'Be something.' And it was." Extraordinary, and exactly right.

This becomes significant for us as we continue to walk our way through the actions of the pre-Bethlehem Christ, because Christ was not only the pre-Bethlehem Christ, as we have seen, but He was also the pre-*everything* Christ, who created all that we see. As we begin to consider His role in creation, perhaps a good place to start is by wondering why it was deemed necessary to create at all—especially since, also as we have seen, the "decree" to create necessitated the "decree" to redeem creation by Jesus's death on the cross. This is clearly not a small issue.

Why Create?

The "why" questions are sometimes the toughest ones because we end up making assumptions that may or may not be correct. With that in mind, we need to start by acknowledging that Genesis 1:1 does *not* begin by saying, "Here's why, in the beginning, God created . . ." We aren't really given the motive behind the creative act—we are simply given the fact of it. But what we know about the God of creation could give us some clues about His motives behind His creating acts. What might have been some reasons for creating?

- **To create strong relationship.** God is a God of relationship who created us for relationship with himself and with one another. The eternal relationship between Father, Son, and Spirit (explored in chapter 2) would, through creation, be extended to creatures intended for that purpose.

- **To create an object to love.** Not only is He a God of relationship but most definitively He is also a God of love (1 John 4:8, 16). While that love could be fully expressed within what C. S. Lewis called the "three-personal God," to create beings to receive that love may have been at the heart of the decree to create.

- **To create as an expression of creativity.** A God of infinite power and infinite wisdom would almost naturally want to express himself in some way. This universe became a platform for the fullest expression of God's infinitely creative heart, mind, and power.

Are those the motives behind the creation of the heavens and the earth? The Scriptures don't specifically tell us. For that reason, perhaps it is best not to overly speculate. Maybe it is best to focus on what the Scriptures *do* tell us about creation and, particularly, the role of the Son in that creative event.

Fully Mysterious

I love mysteries, and the 2017 film production of Agatha Christie's *Murder on the Orient Express* is a classic example of brilliant story-telling. We are presented with the crime and the suspects, and we are allowed to follow the eccentric detective Hercule Poirot as he pursues the clues to the ultimate solution of the mystery. The shock ending leads the watcher to understand why the case was such a challenge—and why the actual solution to the crime was such a surprise.

But perhaps the key idea is solution. I like mysteries because eventually they get solved, and they cease to be mysteries. They become understandable fact. When we began wrestling in this book with the mysteries of eternity past, however, that challenge was conditioned by this ultimate reality: some of the mysteries of the Bible about the nature of the God of creation will not have solutions in this life.

Theologians sometimes refer to God as "the Divine Other" because He defies comprehensive explanation or description. Simply put, He is beyond our reach in some ways. He is Other—"outside" of our categories and "other" than our classifications. Rather than being a source of frustration, this should actually be comforting to us. The fact that God is so big that He is beyond us means He is also bigger than anything we will ever face, and He has committed himself to being our help (Psalm 146:5). That is decidedly good news.

One of the major areas of that "Otherness" is found in the mystery of the Trinity. For millennia, scholars have tried to describe this supernatural reality with natural images like a three-leaf clover or H_2O as water, ice, and vapor—but the results are always, inevitably, unsatisfying. Like the motives for creation, the nature of the "three-personal God" eludes our grasp. In fact, our efforts can be problematic, turning the one-God-in-three-persons into three different gods. Like the mystery of motive, the mystery of the Trinity (affirmed in Matthew 28:19, 1 Peter 1:2, 2 Corinthians 13:14) is best accepted as mystery.

As the three-in-one God worked collaboratively in redemption, this mysterious Godhead also worked together in the event of creation. This understanding begins by acknowledging that creation is a work of God (Psalm 95, Psalm 104, Revelation 4:11) that includes all three persons of the three-in-one God. While our focus here will be on the role of Christ in creation, the Father and the Spirit were also fully engaged.

- Father: "In the beginning God created the heavens and the earth" (Genesis 1:1).

- Spirit: "The earth was formless and void, and darkness was over the surface of the deep, and the Spirit of God was moving over the surface of the waters" (Genesis 1:2).

With that in mind, what do the Scriptures tell us is the role of the Son in creation?

Fully Creator

Maker of All. On a trip to Russia, I visited the massive Moscow flea market at Izmailovsky Park to pick up a few things for our kids. As I looked for something for my daughter, who was in her teens at the time, I found one of the stalls selling handmade Russian dolls in traditional Russian dress. As I looked at one, I noticed that underneath it had a label that proudly affirmed, "Handmade by Tatiana." I asked the man running the stall who Tatiana was, and he said she was his wife! I couldn't pass up that opportunity, so I bought the doll. As I continued to make my way through the flea market, however, I discovered that there were literally dozens of stalls selling that exact doll, and all of them carried the same label—"Handmade by Tatiana." As I had done at the first stall, I asked the men at several of those stalls about Tatiana, and each of them claimed that she was his wife! Obviously, there was a legitimate question as to who had actually made all of those dolls.

There is clearly no such confusion in the Bible about who made the universe we inhabit. The opening parallels between Genesis 1:1 and John 1:1 are stunning. Both begin with "In the beginning." Both deal with the creation of the universe. Both describe God as the Creator who brought all things into being. Where the two accounts diverge is in John's specific naming of the Word (Christ) as the specific person of the three-in-one God who actually did the creating. The beloved apostle wrote:

> In the beginning was the Word, and the Word was with God, and the Word was God. He was in the beginning with God. All things came into being through Him, and apart from Him nothing came into being that has come into being. In Him was life, and the life was the Light of men. (John 1:1–4)

John's conviction was reinforced by the writer of the letter to the Hebrews:

God, after He spoke long ago to the fathers in the prophets in many portions and in many ways, in these last days has spoken to us in His Son, whom He appointed heir of all things, *through whom also He made the world.* And He is the radiance of His glory and the exact representation of His nature, and upholds all things by the word of His power. When He had made purification of sins, He sat down at the right hand of the Majesty on high. (Hebrews 1:1–3; emphasis added)

According to the Genesis account, God created the heavens and the earth. In John's reckoning, the primary agent of creation was Jesus—the living Word. Peter affirms this, writing: "For when they maintain this, it escapes their notice that by the word of God the heavens existed long ago and the earth was formed out of water and by water" (2 Peter 3:5).

The *word* of 2 Peter 3:5 is the same Greek term (*logos*) as was used for *Word* in John 1:1. Jesus is the Word who became flesh (John 1:14) and came to tabernacle in human flesh among His creation. As a result, all of creation comes from Him. Pastor and teacher G. Campbell Morgan wrote:

Wherever the eye rests, whatever the mind is conscious of, is as to first cause the work of Christ. His footprints may be tracked through all creation, and every blush of beauty reveals the touch of His finger. There are no flowers but have in them witness to Him, no marvelous and majestic landscape entrancing the vision of men but that sings the solemn anthem of His power and His beauty. In all the precision of created things, the rolling seasons, the dawn of day, and the westering of the sun, in the emergence of Spring from its garment of Winter, its procedure into the splendor of Summer, and its gorgeous robing in Autumnal glory, is to be discovered the power of the Christ.[1]

Still Engaged with Creation. Many of America's founding fathers were religious but not necessarily Christian. I'm referring to those who were deists, which meant that while they believed in God, they did not see Him as actively involved in creation. He created the universe and got it going, they would contend, then He left it to fend for itself. In writing to the Colossians, Paul told a very different story about both the Creator and His engagement with the universe He made:

> For by Him all things were created, *both* in the heavens and on earth, visible and invisible, whether thrones or dominions or rulers or authorities—all things have been created through Him and for Him. He is before all things, and in Him all things hold together. (Colossians 1:16–17)

In this chapter we've been exploring the fact that Christ created everything. That is no surprise. What would have challenged the deists is the affirmation that He holds everything together (v. 17). This is an active thing. It is an ongoing thing. It is one thing to say that Christ predated creation ("before all things") and that He actually created creation ("all things created through Him and for Him"), but it takes His concern for that creation to an unexpected level when it says that, "in Him all things hold together."

What does that mean? Bible teacher Warren Wiersbe wrote:

> A guide took a group of people through an atomic laboratory and explained how all matter was composed of rapidly moving electric particles. The tourists studied models of molecules and were amazed to learn that matter is made up primarily

of space. During the question period, one visitor asked, "If this is the way matter works, what holds it all together?" For that, the guide had no answer.

But the Christian has an answer: Jesus Christ! Because "He is before all things," He can hold all things together. Again, this is another affirmation that Jesus Christ is God. Only God exists before all of Creation, and only God can make Creation cohere. To make Jesus Christ less than God is to dethrone Him.[2]

Before the world began, Christ was God. Ever since the events of Genesis 1:1 and John 1:1, He is seen as the Creator of the universe—and each of us. Ever since that creation was spoken into existence (2 Peter 3:5), the Savior of the world has been the Sustainer of that world. Even in the moments when that creation rose up in its ultimate rebellion to crucify Jesus, He was—with nail-pierced hands—holding all the creation together.

Fully Redemptive

Long before His earthly experience, the Christ displayed His divine power by His work in creation. That is more than just an important theological fact; it is also an idea that affects how we view His earthly ministry. In our generation we are constantly being told to find the practical application of a biblical text or idea—the "what's in it for me" or "what do I do with this" response mechanism we have been conditioned to expect.

But as legitimate and valuable as that expectation often is, it isn't always the main point. I am convinced that many things are in the Bible for no other reason than to stir in us a sense of wonder at who our God is. Sometimes the "practical takeaway" is nothing more—and nothing less—than calling us to worship God because He deserves it. As former US president Calvin Coolidge wisely said, "It is only when men begin to worship that they begin to grow."

Nowhere is that aspect of Scripture more valid than what we have considered in this chapter. Think about this—with awe and amazement.

Creator among the Created. This is the point John is driving home in the first chapter of his gospel record. His theological prologue to his gospel is on a trajectory, moving toward John 1:14 where we read, "And the Word became flesh, and dwelt among us, and we saw His glory, glory as of the only begotten from the Father, full of grace and truth." The Word (*logos*) came in human form. Everything that follows in John's record is describing what that Word (Jesus) did while walking upon this earth.

As important as that is, however, it only rises to John's intended level when we reckon who that Word was before He came:

- The One who was eternally present with and equal to God (vv. 1–2).

- The One who created all things—and John emphasizes this by repeating "*all* things" (v. 3).

- The One who is the absolute source of all light and life (v. 4).

This is remarkable! To think that the Christ was equal to the Father (see chapter 1) and that He is the maker of heaven and earth and all that is in them is clearly worthy of our attention. But John is driving the greater idea home—*this* is the One who came in human flesh and lived among His created beings. It is something that human beings could have never imagined, yet it is exactly what our God did. In Christ, He came and lived as a human—the uncreated One taking the outward form of a creature. That should inspire us to worship. One day the masses at the throne of God will proclaim: "Worthy is the Lamb that was slain to receive power and riches and wisdom and might and honor and glory and blessing" (Revelation 5:12).

Little Acts of Restoration. In a sense, everything we see in this world that expresses hurt or harm is in opposition to what God designed the world to be. Every disease, every disaster, every death is evidence that something is wrong. Creation, because of human sin, has spun out of orbit and lost its way. By demanding control of our universe, we have made a world that is out of control, and we have proven ever since Genesis 3 our inability to try and bring it under control.

As a result, every miracle Jesus performed was an act of restoring a small piece of the creation that had been ruined by our rebellion. The curse that our first parents initiated with their sin has been wreaking havoc on creation and creature alike ever since. Then Jesus came. As He encountered people damaged by the ravages of creation's brokenness, He healed them. Whether it was restoring sight or sanity, hearing or health, Jesus's miracles were expressions of how God had always intended His creation to be. Whether He was calming a storm or caring for the broken, Jesus's miracles were reminders that He has not abandoned the creatures who abandoned Him.

And not surprisingly, since Jesus was (and is) the Creator, He knew in every situation exactly what was needed to make right what had gone so terribly wrong. He knew not only the depths of this world's need but He was also willing to shoulder that need and—by way of His cross—make restoration possible. For humans, that means restoration to relationship to our Father. For creation, that means restoration to what God's perfect design and creative intent had always desired—an intent that will be perfectly realized when the prophecies of Revelation 21 are fulfilled in time and space.

Once again, we join the restored men and women at the throne of God as they worship, saying, "Worthy are You, our Lord and our God, to receive glory and honor and power; for You created all things, and because of Your will they existed, and were created" (Revelation 4:11).

A Coming Redemption for All Creation. Not only did these miracles display the ultimate restoring power of the Creator but those powerful acts were also anticipations of a day when all creation would experience His full redemption. Our God has no intention of leaving things alone—quite the opposite. He intends to inject himself into the crying, heaving soul of creation and make all things new. To that end, Paul wrote: "For we know that the whole creation groans and suffers the pains of childbirth together until now" (Romans 8:22).

All of this combines to provide us with powerful imagery—the Creator coming to dwell among His created ones and to rescue and repair that creation, which had been broken by sin. This would bring both redemption for humanity and a reversal of the curse on all of creation. The response of that creation will one day be to give to our Creator, Jesus Christ, the worship and honor He so richly deserves. As St. Francis of Assisi taught us to sing:

> All creatures of our God and King,
> Lift up your voice and with us sing,
> Alleluia! Alleluia!
> Thou burning sun with golden beam,
> Thou silver moon with softer gleam!
> O praise Him! O praise Him!

Alleluia! Alleluia! Alleluia!
Let all things their Creator bless,
And worship Him in humbleness,
O praise Him! Alleluia!
Praise, praise the Father, praise the Son,
And praise the Spirit, Three in One!

5

His Appearances in the Old Testament

*Throughout the Old Testament,
Jesus appears by interacting with people and
being pictured by prophecy and symbols.*

Controversial actor and film director Mel Gibson was being interviewed just prior to the release of his 2004 movie *The Passion of the Christ.* When asked what drew him to the story of the crucifixion of Jesus, Gibson responded that he had always loved "hero stories." This had motivated him to make *Braveheart*, the critically acclaimed film about the life and legend of William Wallace, a Scottish patriot who withstood English rule in the Scottish wars of independence during the late thirteenth and early fourteenth centuries. Following several other "hero" stories (including *The Patriot* and *We Were Soldiers*), Gibson said that he wanted to make *The Passion* because the story of Jesus was the greatest hero story of them all. He said, "This is a movie about love, hope, faith and forgiveness. He [Jesus] died for all mankind, suffered for all of us. It's time to get back to that basic message."

I agree. But as we have been seeing together, this greatest hero story of all time has a profound backstory that must inform our appreciation of that hero story; otherwise, Jesus was little more than a martyr dying for a cause, rather than the Savior dying for the world. It should be no surprise, then, that the backstory of this hero story—which, as we have seen, started in eternity past and moved forward to the creation of the universe—extends all the way into the Old Testament. In fact, the backstory of the Christ story is so profoundly embedded into the Scriptures that Bible teachers and scholars, both past and present, readily acknowledge that the entire Bible is *one* story. A story of redemption and rescue, as we have seen.

Martin Luther, the sixteenth-century German reformer who turned the religious world of his day upside down, said this of the Old Testament Scriptures: "Here you find the swaddling cloths and the manger in which Christ lies, and to which the angel points the shepherds (Luke 2:12). Simply and lowly are these swaddling cloths, but dear is the treasure, Christ, who lies in them."

With that in mind, we can begin to see that the Old Testament provides the foundation and the raw materials for the good news of the Savior. It does so by utilizing at least three different instruments for preparing the way for the Messiah's eventual arrival: prophecy and promises, symbols, and Jesus's pre-Bethlehem appearances in the Jewish Scriptures. While many texts could be referenced, some brief examples of each of these three elements will be more than enough to reveal how thoroughly the first testament was preparing the way for Jesus.

Promises and Prophecy

During my lifetime there have been repeated attempts by various Christian leaders to predict the return of Christ—in spite of the fact that Jesus himself said no one but God the Father knows this information (Mark

13:32). While the New Testament gives us absolutely no help whatsoever in determining the timing of Christ's return, it emphatically and repeatedly affirms that He *will* return.

The Old Testament operated in much the same way. The Scriptures continually affirmed—without hinting at a timetable—the certainty of Messiah's eventual arrival. In fact, this is one of the Scriptures' oldest prophecies. I once heard a teacher say that when it comes to understanding the Bible, the first things are of first importance. This is validated by a profound observation made by one of my respected Bible professors in college. He said that every major doctrine of the Bible is found in its root form in Genesis 3. If first things are of first importance, it should come as no surprise that the very first mention of a coming Deliverer is also recorded in Genesis 3.

For those of us who have spent years reading and studying the Bible, the tragic story of Genesis 3 is all too familiar. Having been placed in a perfect environment in which they enjoyed unhindered communion with their Creator and full provision for all they needed in the garden of Eden, our first parents trusted the voice of the deceiver and immediately found all of that perfection badly marred. The warning of a curse was realized. Hiding from God, they also tried to hide from the impact of their disobedience. But their loving God pursued them, and while explaining to them the consequences of their rebellion, He also gave them two gifts.

One gift was that God gave them coverings for their nakedness in order to replace their frail attempts to cover themselves and to relieve their shame and disgrace—at the cost of a life (Genesis 3:21), and the other was that God gave them the first promise of redemption. There would be a Rescuer who would come to deliver them from their failure. This promise was murky and opaque to say the least, but it was nonetheless a prophetic promise intended to give the first couple hope. In Genesis 3:15, while pronouncing judgment upon the deceiver, God also gave this promise to Adam and Eve: "And I will put enmity between you [Satan] and the woman, and between your seed and her seed; He shall bruise you on the head, and you shall bruise him on the heel" (Genesis 3:15).

This promise is referred to by theologians and Bible teachers as the *protevangelium*—the first gospel. Why? Because it brought good news into a world that had just experienced its very first bad news. Warren Wiersbe explained it this way:

> This is the first Gospel declared in the Bible: the good news that the woman's seed (Christ) would ultimately defeat Satan and his seed (Gal. 4:4–5). It is from this point on that the stream divides: Satan and his family (seed) oppose God and His family. God Himself put the enmity (hostility) between them, and God will climax the war when Satan is cast into hell (Rev. 20:10). . . . The OT is the record of the two seeds in conflict; the NT is the record of the birth of Christ and His victory over Satan through the cross.[1]

The spiritual conflict that began in that ancient garden would begin to see its resolution in another garden (Gethsemane) thousands of years later—and between those two gardens, the first where death entered the world and the second where life began to be won, was another prophecy. This promise, tucked away in the dusty pages of the minor prophets, speaks not only of God's coming Deliverer but it also tells where (although, again, not *when*) that Child would be born! In Micah 5:2, we read, "But as for you, Bethlehem

Ephrathah, too little to be among the clans of Judah, from you One will go forth for Me to be ruler in Israel. His goings forth are from long ago, from the days of eternity."

To the people of Israel, Bethlehem (which means, "house of bread") was an important place for two reasons. First, it had been the home of Israel's most beloved king, David the son of Jesse. From the moment the prophet Samuel went to Bethlehem to anoint a king to replace the wayward Saul (1 Samuel 16), Bethlehem would be identified as the "city of David"—a city of kings. Naturally, the expectation was that when Messiah arrived there would be a link to Bethlehem, because Messiah would be David's "greater son." God had promised David that one of his descendants would rule on the throne *forever*. In 2 Samuel 7:12–13, the prophet Nathan delivered God's clear assurance to David, saying:

> When your days are complete and you lie down with your fathers, I will raise up your descendant after you, who will come forth from you, and I will establish his kingdom. He shall build a house for My name, and I will establish the throne of his kingdom forever.

While that promise was immediately fulfilled in the birth of Solomon, the forever piece of the promise would be discovered in the birth of Christ. One result of this promise was that the title "Son of David"—a title often used of Jesus in the Gospels—became the equivalent of "Messiah." Bethlehem is the legacy home behind all of those important ideas.

The second critical importance of Bethlehem was that it was the home of the "shepherds' fields." We know this from Luke 2:8, of course, but historians tell us that one of the main purposes of these flocks of sheep was that many of them were specifically raised to be used as sacrifices at the temple in Jerusalem. Because the ritual sacrifices (especially Passover, which we will see next) required the offering of lambs, the shepherds' fields were significant. And for Bethlehem—the site of those fields—to be the birthplace of Jesus, the Lamb of God who would take away the sins of the world (John 1), is only fitting and appropriate.

The promises and prophecies that revealed that God would provide a Deliverer became a critical part of the Old Testament backstory to the Christmas story and the story of Christ, the Messiah. He was the Seed of the woman, and He was born in Bethlehem.

Symbols and Pictures

We live in a symbol-driven world. As I was growing up, when I saw a skull-and-crossbones, I knew it meant something was poisonous. Today there are symbols that warn of extreme danger from nuclear or hazardous waste. International travelers who journey to lands where they don't speak the local language find signage in international airports that help them navigate their way through the unfamiliar territory. On a more individual note, text messages are dominated by emojis, the small symbols that describe everything from emotions to activities to sports teams to countries to . . . well, you name it. These cartoonlike symbols have become a substantial part of communication in the digital world.

The use of symbols to express significant ideas also has deep roots in the Old Testament Scriptures—and the most dramatic of these symbols pointed to the Christ who would come as Israel's Messiah and the world's Savior. Although there is an expansive list of such symbols (tabernacle, rock from which water was drawn, the sacrifice for a cleansed leper, and more), one will be sufficient for our purposes as we see the Old Testament as, in Martin Luther's words, the "swaddling clothes" of the Christ.

The Passover Lamb. Some of the deep traditions of Judaism were born before Israel had even become a nation at Mount Sinai. When Moses returned from the mountains of Midian to be God's spokesman to Pharaoh and the leader of the Hebrews' exodus from slavery, a series of ten miraculous displays demonstrated the power and authority of God to call His people home. Each of these deeds carried substantial symbolism in its own right, but none so clearly pointed to the coming Christ as the Passover lamb.

The tenth and final of those power displays was what we call Passover. After warning of death to the firstborn throughout Egypt (Exodus 11:4–6), the Lord clearly described the remedy for rescue. How could a family escape that sweeping judgment? A sacrificial lamb would take the place of the firstborn—much like the ram that had been provided to Abraham on Mount Moriah as a substitute for Isaac so many years before (Genesis 22). The instructions were carefully described:

> Speak to all the congregation of Israel, saying, "On the tenth of this month they are each one to take a lamb for themselves, according to their

fathers' households, a lamb for each household."
(Exodus 12:3)

"Your lamb shall be an unblemished male a year
old; you may take it from the sheep or from the
goats." (Exodus 12:5)

"Moreover, they shall take some of the blood and
put it on the two doorposts and on the lintel of the
houses in which they eat it." (Exodus 12:7)

"The blood shall be a sign for you on the houses
where you live; and when I see the blood I will
pass over you, and no plague will befall you to
destroy you when I strike the land of Egypt."
(Exodus 12:13)

The New Testament not only sees the Passover
lamb as a symbol of divine rescue but it also sees the
lamb as a picture of Christ himself. Paul wrote, "Clean
out the old leaven so that you may be a new lump, just
as you are in fact unleavened. For Christ our Passover
also has been sacrificed" (1 Corinthians 5:7).

"Christ our Passover" reinforces this symbolism—and it is no coincidence that Christ was crucified during the Feast of the Passover. Bible historians

estimate that up to a quarter of a million lambs were sacrificed each year during the Passover season. It makes absolute sense that at such a time the Lamb of God who came to take away the sins of the world would also be offered.

People and Presence

Above all else, the Old Testament is a true story—actually a collection of true stories that combine to create the one big story. Since the purpose of that story is to point to Jesus, it is reasonable that the people in that story would cause us to lift our eyes so we would look forward to the coming, promised Christ.

To that end, Pastor Tim Keller of New York's Redeemer Presbyterian Church, among others, sees hints, whispers, and anticipations throughout the Old Testament of Jesus as the "true and better" representation of what we see in an encyclopedia of biblical personalities. Adam, Abel, Abraham, Isaac, Joseph, and many others are all important in the narrative, and their individual stories have great value and significance in their own right. But there is more, as Keller says:

Jesus is the true and better Adam who passed the test in the garden and whose obedience is imputed to us.

Jesus is the true and better Abel who, though innocently slain, has blood now that cries out, not for our condemnation, but for acquittal.

Jesus is the true and better Abraham who answered the call of God to leave all the comfortable and familiar and go out into the void not knowing wither he went to create a new people of God.

Jesus is the true and better Isaac who was not just offered up by his father on the mount but was truly sacrificed for us. And when God said to Abraham, "Now I know you love me because you did not withhold your son, your only son whom you love from me," now we can look at God taking his son up the mountain and sacrificing him and say, "Now we know that you love us because you did not withhold your son, your only son, whom you love from us."

Keller continues through eight other biblical figures, declaring at the end, "The Bible's really not about you—it's about him"—Jesus.[2]

In the cases of these and other Old Testament figures, elements of their stories point us forward to a "true and better" fulfillment in Jesus's redemption story. The threads of the "smaller stories" of the Bible all feed into the true and better story of the Rescuer that God sent to restore us to a right relationship with our Creator. When we see all of those threads woven into the fabric of redemptive grace, it transforms the way we understand the Gospels and the Savior to whom they bear witness. Talk about a backstory!

Not only is Jesus anticipated in the characters of the Old Testament story but Bible scholars also believe that Jesus himself steps onto the pages of OT Scriptures in what theologians call "theophanies" or "Christophanies." These words find their roots in the Greek term *phaneroo*, which speaks of something being revealed (like our word *epiphany*), and they describe Christ (or God) appearing or being revealed. In these events, scholars believe that the Christ makes pre-Bethlehem appearances on the earth and interacts with people in specific ways and at specific times.

It must be accepted that since the Bible doesn't clearly define these events as Christophanies, these are easily the most speculative of the Old Testament road signs pointing to Jesus. Despite their speculative nature, some of these events are very interesting and at least deserve a mention. They include the following:

Melchizedek (Genesis 14). The priest and king of peace to whom Abraham paid tithes may have been a Christophany, for the writer of Hebrews affirmed that Christ was a priest of the order of Melchizedek (Hebrews 5:5–6).

Abraham's visitor (Genesis 18). Three strangers, two of whom are later described as angels, appear at Abraham's tent prior to the destruction of Sodom and Gomorrah. The third visitor, with whom Abraham sought to negotiate a withholding of judgment, is seen as Christ by many scholars.

An Angel (Genesis 32). When Jacob wrestled all night with an angel (Hosea 12:4), it is believed that perhaps this "angel" (which, again, means "messenger") was Christ in physical form before Bethlehem.

Commander of the Lord's armies (Joshua 5:13–15). As Joshua prepared for the battles by which the promised land would be won, he encountered a stranger with a drawn sword. Joshua was told (as was Moses at the burning bush) to take off his shoes—he was on holy ground! That instruction would not likely be given in the presence of a mere man or angel.

"Son of the gods" (Daniel 3). When Shadrach, Meshach, and Abednego refused to worship Nebuchadnezzar's image, they were cast into a fiery furnace as punishment for their rebellion. When Nebuchadnezzar looked into the furnace, however, he saw with them a fourth person— whom he described as looking like "a son of the gods" (Daniel 3:25).

While there are other examples, these are a few of the Old Testament events where Jesus may have appeared in bodily form before His arrival in the flesh at Bethlehem. Combined with all of the other evidence we have seen, the Old Testament clearly provides us with a wide variety of opportunities to anticipate the promised Messiah and what He would be like—the perfect Son displayed in a variety of imperfect images that could never fully express who He is.

Messianic Hope

When Mel Gibson said that *The Passion of the Christ* was a film about, among other things, hope, he could not have been more correct. The Old Testament backstory to the story of the cross generated the most intense kind of hope for the covenant people of God. The sum total of the prophecies and promises provided in their ancient Scriptures created within the people of Israel an expectation that a Rescuer was coming.

Although the Jewish people expected a radically different kind of Messiah than Jesus would be, they nevertheless believed that Messiah would come. This Jewish messianic expectation was grounded in generations of anticipation, but their expectations were conditioned by how they read the prophecies and how they understood their history.

> Seen in the Torah: Deuteronomy 18:15 had them expecting a **prophet**:
>> "The LORD your God will raise up for you a prophet like me from among you, from your countrymen, you shall listen to him."

> Seen in the Psalms: Psalm 2 and Psalm 110 had them expecting a **conqueror**:

"I will surely tell of the decree of the LORD: He said to Me, 'You are My Son, today I have begotten You. Ask of Me, and I will surely give the nations as Your inheritance, and the very ends of the earth as Your possession. You shall break them with a rod of iron, You shall shatter them like earthenware.' " (Psalm 2:7–9)

The LORD says to my Lord: "Sit at My right hand until I make Your enemies a footstool for Your feet." (Psalm 110:1)

Seen in the prophets: Isaiah 9 had them expecting a **ruler**:

For a child will be born to us, a son will be given to us; and the government will rest on His shoulders; and His name will be called Wonderful Counselor, Mighty God, Eternal Father, Prince of Peace. There will be no end to the increase of His government or of peace, on the throne of David and over his kingdom, to establish it and to uphold it with justice and righteousness from then on and forevermore. The zeal of the LORD of hosts will accomplish this. (Isaiah 9:6–7)

These expectations seemed to be affirmed when Judah "The Hammer" Maccabeus led a revolt against Assyrian oppressors (167–160 BC). The Assyrians had desecrated the altar in Jerusalem, leading Judah and his brothers to raise an army and drive the oppressors out of the land. Then the temple was cleansed and restored—an event that is still commemorated every year (ironically around the same time of year Christmas is observed) in Hanukkah, the festival of lights.

The resulting Hasmonean dynasty ruled for decades—until Rome arose. Israel was conquered and dominated once more. Clearly, this was not the rule or the rescue God had promised. The chosen people were looking for the wrong kind of king. As one poet said:

> They all were looking for a king
> To raise them up and lift them high;
> Thou camest a little baby thing
> That made a young girl cry.

Yes, Messiah would conquer and would rule and would prophesy, but not in the ways the people expected. Why? Because when the true Messiah arrived, it would not be to deliver political or national freedom. He would come to provide hope—real, lasting, eternal hope. In 1847, Adolphe Charles Adam wrote of this supreme hope in his classic French Christmas song "Cantique de Noel," which John Sullivan Dwight translated into the well-known "O Holy Night."

> O holy night, the stars are brightly shining,
> It is the night of the dear Savior's birth;
> Long lay the world in sin and error pining,
> 'Till he appeared and the soul felt its worth.
> *A thrill of hope*, the weary world rejoices,
> For yonder breaks a new and glorious morn;
> Fall on your knees, Oh hear the angel voices!
> O night divine! O night when Christ was born.
> O night, O holy night, O night divine.

6

His Announced Arrival

The final preparations
for Jesus's coming were delivered
in angelic announcements
to two unlikely people.

Our family had gathered together, which always involves lots of food and lots of catching up. Our youngest son and his wife arrived early, and he immediately told his mom that he wanted to pray for the meal when the time came. While not totally off the radar, it was nonetheless a bit surprising for Mark to so strongly request to offer the prayer. When the time came, Mark began to choke up as he prayed and thanked God for his wife, Amy, and the opportunities the Lord was providing for them. Then, as he thanked the Lord for His many blessings, he paused and gave thanks for the child who would be born to them in several months. This was a genuine and sincere prayer, but it was also a surprising way to announce to us that he and Amy were expecting. It certainly spiced up our family gathering!

Depending upon the circumstances, announcements can be either a curse or a blessing. I remember the languid boredom of the first moments of my school days as the school principal would drone on and on over the public address system of the day's announcements. In my twenty-plus years as a pastor, announcements were generally considered a necessary evil in a worship service—the black hole that distracted from whatever the theme of that service was intended to be. I understand how valuable these updates on church life can be, but to me they usually felt like a disruption to the ideas I wanted the service to communicate.

On the other hand, wedding announcements are times for celebration and excitement. Birth announcements cause us to reflect on the gift of life. Graduation announcements applaud a task completed and the start of a new phase of life. Political figures announce their candidacy for office, companies announce stock issues, studios announce new movie releases, and the list goes on. Clearly, announcements can be significant declarations of key moments in life.

Nowhere, however, has there ever been a more important announcement in human history than the long-awaited announcement that the promised Messiah would finally arrive. In one sense, it could be said that, as we have seen, the entire Old Testament was a slow and patient notification that Messiah would come—but two angelic visits mentioned early in two of the Gospels would be intensely more dramatic. They would tell the two principal people in the Christmas story that not only was Messiah's time at hand but also that they would be entrusted with His care, training, and preparation. And the people receiving these special announcements could not have been more unlikely.

An Impossible Story

Over the years, I have come across several fascinating statements of impossibility from history:

"These guys will never last. Guitar groups are on their way out." (Decca Records rejecting an audition tape from the Beatles in 1962.)

"There is no way that we will lose to the Jets." (Stated by a Baltimore Colts player prior to the 1969 Super Bowl, which they lost 16–7 to the Joe Namath–led New York Jets.)

"It is not possible that the Allied forces will invade in this weather." (Attributed to a German officer on June 6, 1944—D Day—and the turning point in World War II.)

"How can this be, since I am a virgin?" (Mary's response to the angel Gabriel after he announces that she will give birth to the Christ.)

The difference between these statements of impossibility is that the first three are all resolved by human answers, but the fourth has no human explanation. What we see in these familiar words that precede the Christmas story would be a startling, exhilarating, humbling, terrifying, impossible message for Mary— much like the one received by her fiancé, Joseph. By its very definition *impossible* is impossible! It lies outside our categories and defies our attempts at explanation. It calls us to look beyond the natural to the power of One who is supernatural, or above and beyond nature.

As we are reminded of these familiar words and events, what we see is a building case of impossibilities. To see it, I want us to look at the announcements to Mary and Joseph in tandem, so we can grasp a bit of the impossibility they were being asked to accept.

But before we look at the common threads of impossibility that weave their way through these two announcements, what are the distinctive elements that separate them?

Separate Tracks, Same Story

When we place the announcements of Jesus's incarnation beside one another, the differences are clearly seen, and they serve specific purposes—in some cases, defined by the intent of the author and the audience to whom they were writing.

Introduction of the announcement. In Matthew 1, the writer of that gospel begins with what many Bible readers dread and seek to avoid—a genealogy. But this is not a throwaway item. Far from it. Matthew is the most Jewish of the Gospels, and since the Messiah would be defined as the "Son of David," that line and heritage must be on the table from the outset. For Luke, however, the connection between Messiah and His prophesied forerunner, John the Baptist, was the necessary starting point. Make no mistake, however. Luke also understands the vital importance of heritage and includes his own record of Christ's genealogy in Luke 3 (and mentions the connection to David in Luke 1:27). But for Luke and his audience, introduction to the "Elijah" character prophesied by Malachi took precedence.

Mary and Joseph's state of mind. This is really important. When the messenger angel Gabriel comes to Mary, the message and the messenger are completely unanticipated. She has no background or preparation for this moment, so although she is perplexed (Luke 1:29) by this event, emotionally, she is a *tabula rasa*—a blank slate. Also, the promises of Messiah were of such renown in ancient Israel that, as Elizabeth would confirm to Mary (Luke 1:42–45), being the woman who would give birth to the Deliverer would be the honor of a lifetime—a dream come true. By contrast, Joseph is in deep despair (Matthew 1:19–20). His entire life has been brought to ruin by the news that Mary is pregnant. His fiancée, by all human appearances, is an unfaithful young woman, bearing the child of another man. Mary's dream was Joseph's nightmare. As a result, the angels' messages have very different emotional impacts on the young couple. For Mary, Gabriel's message is one of humbling honor; but for Joseph, the message he received is one of comfort and assurance.

Evidence of the angel's claim. For Mary, this impossible announcement has her a little sideways—so the angel offers proof. How could such a miraculous event take place in her life and in her virgin womb (Luke 1:34)? Just as a miraculous conception had taken place in the life and aged womb of her relative, Elizabeth (Luke 1:36–37), a miraculous conception of a far different kind occurred with Mary. By contrast, Joseph is offered no evidence of the messenger's claim that Mary's child is born of God—he is just expected to believe it. Perhaps that call to faith is the perfect evidence that Joseph was, as Matthew said, a "righteous man" (Matthew 1:19)—that is, a man in right relationship with his God.

Missional focus. Both messages present a Child who will accomplish great things. The results of those great things, however, are presented as very different. For Mary, the message is that this Child will be David's greater Son who will rule as king forever (Luke 1:32–33). Joseph's missional message is that Jesus "will save His people from their sins" (Matthew 1:21). Those distinctive messages dovetail, of course, because Jesus's sacrifice for sins prepares the way for God's eternal kingdom. But the focus of what this Son would do is different in the two messages.

Their immediate responses. Mary's response was to travel to the home of Elizabeth and spend time with her (Luke 1:39–40). We aren't told why she went, but some speculate that she was seeking to avoid the wagging tongues in Nazareth that have targeted her as a sinful young woman. Others think she is going to Elizabeth to see with her own eyes the evidence the angel had offered—that Elizabeth really was pregnant in her old age. Joseph, however, simply responds by obeying the angelic messenger. He puts aside any thoughts of divorce and takes Mary "as his wife" (Matthew 1:24).

These differences are important, for they remind us that though Mary and Joseph are participants in the same eternity-changing story, they are also individuals on individual tracks. They are moving onto the stage of the most important drama in human history—and they are entering the story with their own emotional challenges and expectations.

It is virtually impossible for any of us to understand completely what this young couple was being asked to believe, accept, and embrace. The sheer weight of what was being said and what that message implied would have been overwhelming to the extreme. Yet, these individually distinct pieces of the messages Mary and Joseph received showed afresh the individual cost and promise the couple was offered. G. Campbell Morgan wrote:

> This is the biblical interpretation of the person of Jesus. A naturalistic philosophy necessarily cannot accept this as true. Then that philosophy is called upon to account for Jesus some other way—and the only way to do that is to do what naturalistic philosophy does, change the Jesus that is presented in the New Testament. To deny the

supernatural origin of Jesus is to make Him natural merely. To do that invalidates the records, not
of His Being alone, but of His teaching and His
power in human history. . . . But we are not among
the number of those who hold this philosophy of
God. We do not think of Him as imprisoned
within the laws that we have discovered, and the
forces we know.[1]

However, as different as they are, the two announcements have profound similarities—lacing together the
two announcements into one extraordinary reality.
The time has come for God's promises to be fulfilled.

Same Story, Same Truths

In the late 1980s, Marlene and I packed up our four
small children and our possessions, left my hometown
in West Virginia where I had pastored for the previous
eight years, and like the Clampetts of the old *Beverly
Hillbillies* TV show headed to Southern California. I
had accepted a pastoral position in the Los Angeles
suburb of Carson, and we would settle into our little
house in north Long Beach. While there, in addition

to the pastoral work, I enrolled in a master's degree program at Talbot School of Theology. We had a wonderful church family, and the educational benefits I received at Talbot dramatically altered my approach to and appreciation of the Scriptures. To say that our three years there were a whirlwind would be to vastly undervalue the power of a whirlwind.

Now, some thirty years later, Marlene and I will occasionally catch a news report or a segment in a TV program where familiar scenes from the South Bay area of Los Angeles County will remind us of memories from long ago. In that moment, either Marlene or I will almost instinctively ask, "Did we really live there, or did I just dream that?" It seems impossible, but as we begin to revisit our memories in the LA Basin, those common threads of shared experience help to reaffirm a reality that has somewhat been blurred by the passing of time.

For Mary and Joseph, I wonder if something similar might have been their experience. During the nine months of pregnancy or the childhood years leading up to Jesus's appearance in Jerusalem's temple at age twelve, did they individually wonder if they had imagined it all? Had the angel really visited them? If so, sharing again the common themes of their individual messages could have been just the anchor they needed to keep the impossible clearly in view. What were those common themes?

"Don't be afraid!" What could be more appropriate than this? Among the first words of the angelic messenger to Mary (Luke 1:30) and to Joseph (Matthew 1:20) is the expression of peace that would be characteristic of Jesus's interactions with His disciples. Over and over, in times of stress and struggle, Jesus would say to them, "Don't be afraid" or "Peace be with you." Particularly, it was a significant theme of Jesus's teaching to His followers on the night before the cross. There, in the midst of the turmoil and confusion the disciples were experiencing, Jesus wove words of peace throughout what we call the Upper Room Discourse:

- "Do not let your heart be troubled; believe in God, believe also in Me" (John 14:1).

- "Peace I leave with you; My peace I give to you; not as the world gives do I give to you. Do not let your heart be troubled, nor let it be fearful" (John 14:27).

- "These things I have spoken to you, so that in
  Me you may have peace. In the world you have
  tribulation, but take courage; I have overcome
  the world" (John 16:33).

This should not come as a surprise to us. Nothing
could be more fitting than for the announcement of
the coming of the Prince of Peace (Isaiah 9:6) to be
comfortably lodged in the offer of peace to the young
couple receiving that message. For Mary, that peace
was buttressed by two important realities enveloped in
the angel's promise of peace:

- **"Favored one" (Luke 1:28).** The word *favored*
  finds its root in the Greek word *charis*, which
  means "grace." The entire purpose of the
  incarnation was to bring into the world the
  Christ who would be "full of grace and truth,"
  yet it begins with a woman finding grace
  with God! Keep in mind that *grace* means
  "undeserved favor." Mary was a human being,
  and even the expression of God's blessing to her
  regarding the birth of Christ is couched in the
  terms of "grace"—undeserved favor.

- **"The Lord is with you" (Luke 1:28).** This is wonderfully similar to the Lord's promise to Gideon in Judges 6:12 where he was told, "The LORD is with you." The point? God is calling Mary to an amazing and overwhelming task, but He himself is with her, so she can be assured of His help in carrying out this responsibility.

Mary's peace finds strength in the God who supplies both His grace and His presence. For Joseph, the offer of peace is more pragmatic. Torn by the news of Mary's pregnancy, Joseph contemplates his options, and they are not pleasant to ponder. The ancient penalties for adultery were severe.

- Egypt: cut off the person's nose
- Persia: cut off the nose and one ear
- Israel: death by stoning (Deuteronomy 22:22–23)

In ancient Israel, this was a capital crime. Joseph is confronted with a massive problem—what should he do?

1. He has the right to divorce her and have her killed. But notice that he is more concerned

with mercy than with justice. He is like the
God he serves in that he is just—yet merciful.

2. He has the heart to seek other action. That is
the definition of mercy: to seek another's best
rather than selfishly exercising personal rights.

Imagine the turmoil in his heart. Rather than celebrating his coming wedding to the young woman as he had anticipated for years, now the best way he can show love to her is to spare her life and spare her the shame of a public divorce. He decides to put her away "secretly." He cares too much to see her put on public display, so he settles on a simple solution—two witnesses and no declaration of cause for the divorce. But whatever he does, he can't just walk away.

Here we see a characteristic of Joseph that is both profound and wonderful. Although he is just a poor, hardworking man in the midst of great heartache and disappointment, he shows a merciful heart governed by restraint and self-sacrifice.

Now we see why Joseph has been chosen for this task—he who would be a "father" to the Son of God reflects some of the greatest attributes of the heart of the Father himself. Caring, compassionate, loving, merciful—God uses the good heart of Joseph to protect Mary and her unborn child when others might have offered her up for stoning.

Into this season of struggle, the angel speaks words of peace. It is as if he said, "Fear not, Joseph. Don't hesitate to take her as your wife. God is at work in ways you can't understand. Just know this—there is nothing to fear."

Peace—even in the announcement of the arrival of the Prince of Peace.

The work of the Spirit. The Holy Spirit would creatively bring about the physical conception of Jesus. Why was this necessary? Not just because Mary was a virgin and needed to be made pregnant. In the conception that occurs in a womb between a man and a woman, a new life is brought into being. But that was not the case with Christ who, as God, was eternally preexistent (as we have seen).

Similarly, the angel asks Joseph to believe in more than the virgin birth. He is challenging Joseph to believe in a virginal conception! He says, in effect, "You're right. The child is not your son; He is God's Son."

A Son. For Mary, the title *Son* would have been very significant. In Semitic thought, a son was seen as a "carbon copy" of his father, so that the phrase "son of" was often used to refer to one who possessed his father's qualities. To say that her baby was "Son of the Most High" (Luke 1:32) was to grant Him the status of equality with Yahweh and was, without question, a declaration of Jesus's deity! Furthermore, His divine sonship is linked to His Messiahship. In Luke 1:32–33, Gabriel's announcement makes it clear that Jesus the Son of the Most High will perform the role of the promised Messiah—to one day rule and reign on the throne of David, as we see next.

Son of David. The promise of the throne of David is the fulfillment of the Davidic Covenant (2 Samuel 7:13–16) and of the messianic reign described in Isaiah 9:6–7. The angel promises that the reign of Christ over the nation of Israel as her true King would continue into eternity.

The key is that David had understood that these things referred not just to the immediate son (Solomon) who would build the temple but even more so to the future Son who would rule forever. As a Jewish girl who had lived her entire life in the anticipation of the coming Messiah, there could have been no question of what the angel was promising. And this was confirmed by the words heard by Joseph, son of David. Because Joseph was in the Davidic line and in line for the throne, the reason for the genealogy of Matthew 1 is validated—legitimizing the right of Joseph's Heir to the throne of Israel's ancient and greatest king.

Name Him Jesus. In Luke 1:31, Mary was told to "name Him Jesus," and in Matthew 1:21, Joseph was instructed to "call His name Jesus," the name that means "Jehovah is Savior." Joseph was specifically told, "You shall call His name Jesus" because in Jewish culture, naming a child is the task of the father. Joseph, standing in the heavenly Father's stead, would make this declaration—and in so doing he would do more than merely provide the Child's name. He would also define the mission of the miraculously born Baby. Jesus would save, and He would save from sin (v. 21).

And with that, the loop of biblical promise is complete. Looking all the way back to the garden of our first parents' failure, remembering the promise that the woman's Seed would destroy our true, spiritual Enemy and set us free from the consequences of our rebellion—that promise would now be ensconced in human flesh. That rescue was now arriving. As someone has put it: "The Son of God became the Son of man so that sons of men could become the sons of God."

The Backstory for the Same Story

With these announcements, the preparations that began in eternity past are concluded. The nine months of pregnancy have begun, but on a human level only because this young couple had willingly received and believed the announcement of the remarkable birth in which they would participate.

The message of the angel to Mary is a message to us as well. It is certainly a call to worship, and it is a call to embrace the matchless grace that Jesus would bring to Mary and the whole world. But perhaps for us it is a call to faith in a mighty God . . .

> Whose *power* is unstoppable,
> Whose *strength* is inconceivable,
> Whose *supply* is immeasurable,
> Whose *might* is undeniable.

And what of Joseph? I would suggest that Joseph is a marvelous character who . . .

Teaches us to respond to hurt with restraint;
Teaches us to respond to disappointment with
    mercy;
Teaches us to trust God's love and compassion.

I would submit to you that the little carpenter shop in Nazareth was a pretty special place to be—in part because of the character of Joseph. Though we never hear him speak, his life speaks volumes about a heart for God. Here is how Herbert Lockyer characterizes Joseph:

Tenderly he cared for his dear one as if the Child she was bearing were his own. Overawed by the mystery of it all, that his beloved Mary had been chosen as the mother of the Lord he as a devout Jew had eagerly anticipated, we can imagine how he would superintend every detail of the Nativity.

What holy thoughts must have filled the mind of Mary's guardian. Where suspicion regarding Mary's purity once lurked, strong faith now reigned as he looked into the lovely face of Mary's Child. At last God's promises had been fulfilled and before him was the Babe through whom God's covenants would be established.[2]

This is what the angel had announced, and it is what Mary and Joseph had embraced. I trust that we will likewise embrace this wonderful, extraordinary, peace-giving good news as well. May we respond to the following Christmas announcement, which celebrates eternity's great invitation, with the same openness that Mary and Joseph responded to their notice about Jesus's birth.

> O come, all ye faithful
> Joyful and triumphant
> O come ye, o come ye to Bethlehem
> Come and behold Him
> Born the King of Angels!
> O come, let us adore Him
> O come, let us adore Him
> O come, let us adore Him
> Christ the Lord.

CONCLUSION

The Christmas Story

Joseph also went up from Galilee, from the city of Nazareth, to Judea, to the city of David which is called Bethlehem, because he was of the house and family of David, in order to register along with Mary, who was engaged to him, and was with child. While they were there, the days were completed for her to give birth. And she gave birth to her firstborn son; and she wrapped Him in cloths, and laid Him in a manger, because there was no room for them in the inn. (Luke 2:4–7)

And so we arrive at Christmas—the most wonderful time of the year. But this wonderful time was not an overnight happening or a sudden intervention. The arrival of Messiah Jesus was an eternity in the making, coming to us and for us in "the fullness of time" (Galatians 4:4).

What an extraordinary thing it is to consider that the timeless One, who for all eternity existed outside the realm of time, would enter time in the fullness of time to bring eternity to us. This is the Christmas story, but as we have seen, it is not a dot on a line—it is the line itself! This is the story that reaches back into eternity past to show the plans and purposes of the Father and the Son, and it reaches forward to the cross and the resurrection, and into eternity future.

One day (an inescapable reference to time), there will be no more time because the eternal Hero will have come. On that day, we will realize that for which we were created—for "He has also set eternity in their heart" (Ecclesiastes 3:11), and the long desires of our hearts will finally be realized. In the meantime, we live day-to-day and by His grace. C. S. Lewis is purported to have said: "The future is something which everyone reaches at the rate of 60 minutes an hour, whatever he does, whoever he is."

Those hours and days and months and years all point us to Jesus and to the eternity He came to purchase. Our sense of anticipation and expectation grows as we grow closer to Him and to that promised eternity. And as we anticipate, we celebrate "the most wonderful time of the year."

Notes

Chapter 1. His Character as God

[1] A. W. Tozer, *The Knowledge of the Holy* (New York: Harper and Row, 1961), 9.

[2] D. Martyn Lloyd-Jones, *The Life of Joy* (London: Hodder, 1989), 148.

Chapter 2. His Relationship with the Father

[1] Kenneth Bailey, *Paul Through Mediterranean Eyes* (Downers Grove, IL: IVP Academic, 2011), 110–111.

[2] Raymond Brown, *The Yale Anchor Bible* (New Haven, CT: Yale University Press, 1970), 772.

[3] Gary Burge, *The Bible Knowledge Background Commentary: John's Gospel* (Wheaton, IL: Victor Books, 2005), 100.

Chapter 3. His Preparation for the Cross

[1] Stanley Toussaint, *The Bible Knowledge Commentary (New Testament)* (Wheaton, IL: Victor Books, 1983), 358.

[2] R. N. Longenecker, *The Expositor's Bible Commentary*, vol. 9 (Grand Rapids, MI: Zondervan, 1981), 279.

Chapter 4. His Role as Creator

[1] G. Campbell Morgan, *A First Century Message to a Twentieth Century Christian* (Edinburgh, Scotland: Crossreach Publications, 2016), 193.

[2] Warren Wiersbe, *Be Complete* (Wheaton, IL: Victor Books, 1981), 61.

Chapter 5. His Appearances in the Old Testament

[1] Warren Wiersbe, *Wiersbe's Expository Outlines on the Old Testament* (Covington, KY: Calvary Book Room, 1968), 26–27.

[2] Tim Keller, *Preaching: Communicating Faith in an Age of Skepticism* (Westminster, London, England: Penguin Books, 2015), 77–78.

Chapter 6. His Announced Arrival

[1] G. Campbell Morgan, *The Gospel According to Luke* (Grand Rapids, MI: Fleming H. Revell, 1986), 24.

[2] Herbert Lockyer, *All the Men of the Bible* (Grand Rapids, MI: Zondervan, 1958), 203.

Help us get the word out!

Our Daily Bread Publishing exists to feed the soul with the Word of God.

If you appreciated this book, please let others know.

- Pick up another copy to give as a gift.
- Share a link to the book or mention it on social media.
- Write a review on your blog, on a book-seller's website, or at our own site (odb.org/store).
- Recommend this book for your church, book club, or small group.

Connect with us:

 @ourdailybread

@ourdailybread

@ourdailybread

Our Daily Bread Publishing
PO Box 3566
Grand Rapids, Michigan 49501 USA

✉ books@odb.org